A
Compassionate
Civilization

A
Compassionate
Civilization

The Urgency of Sustainable Development and Mindful
Activism - Reflections and Recommendations

Robertson Work

ISBN: 1546972617
ISBN 13: 9781546972617
Library of Congress Control Number: 2017908618
CreateSpace Independent Publishing Platform
North Charleston, South Carolina

Advance Praise for *A Compassionate Civilization*

"In this book, Robertson Work has uniquely combined idealism, personal commitment, the whole system analysis, and practical tools to make our world free, fair, and just. *A Compassionate Civilization* is a very persuasive call for transformation to ensure environmental sustainability, gender equality, justice, participatory governance, cultural tolerance, and peace and nonviolence. Professor Work's holistic, multidisciplinary analysis of the 'Movement of Movements,' innovative leadership methods, and four faces of war and peace has reminded us all about contributions we can make as caring global citizens through social and political activism to bring about change. I strongly recommend this book for students, activists, scholars, political leaders, and citizens of the world."

- Shabbir Cheema, PhD, senior fellow, East-West Center, Honolulu, Hawaii; former UNDP Director of Management Development and Governance

"This luminous book is both a magnificent testimony as well as a profound guidance for those who want to make a better world, in fact, help create a compassionate civilization. It is written by a man who has given his life to the heartfelt and creative work of human and cultural growth in over 50 countries. Thus, it is a superb work of courage and skill, practical knowhow, and the ingenious gifts of one who is sourced in spirit. To read this inspired book is to be called to one's greater life in both soul craft and world making. It is to be evoked to bring one's all to the deepest issues and possibilities of our time."

-   Jean Houston, PhD, author, *A Passion for the Possible*

"Robertson Work's book is a personal testament about wrestling with, and responding to, the urgent challenges of our times. He then dares to share his practical steps to make good on the promise. The book is also an invitation to us, the readers, to enter into a 'multilogue' with him and everyone else as we give shape to our own declarations, strategies, and action. This is the true power of the book. While *A Compassionate Civilization* sets a context, only we personally can decide the implications it has for living our own unique and unrepeatable lives."

-   Terry D. Bergdall, PhD, professor and author; former president and CEO, Institute of Cultural Affairs, USA

"In his book, *A Compassionate Civilization*, Robertson Work states a comprehensive overview of the dangers of civilization continuing on the path of greed as it is manifest in disregard of our planet and of the 99 percent of the world's population. But he also issues a hope-filled call to action and a road map for creating the compassionate civilization. He is the perfect person to write this book, which combines the purpose and the path of his life."

-   Joy Sloan Jinks, MSW, community organizer, founder of Swamp Gravy, Georgia's Folk-Life Play, author of *Dynamic Aging*

"Rob offers us a new social philosophy, which is both visionary and pragmatic, both individual and collective. Its call is just as urgent as our next breath. I give wise attention to Rob's insights based on his real-world experience. His message is beyond the snares of social ideologies now revealed as inadequate. I salute him for his brilliance, courage, and continued hopeful presence and receive his book's manifestation as a noble gift, urgent yet timeless in character and depth."

- Larry Ward, PhD, dharma teacher in the Thich Nhat Hanh tradition of practice and Director of The Lotus Institute

"A rare man of wisdom who walks his talk, Robertson shares years of experience as a professional in international affairs, whose essential goal is relieving suffering. He offers a compelling integral vision of compassionate civilizational transformation, while encouraging the reader to participate in cocreation and asking compelling questions like 'What are you willing to die for?' Filled with inspiring words, he weaves a compelling story of the possible future we all yearn for and how we can get there."

- Nancy Roof, Editor, *Kosmos* journal, www.kosmos journal.org

"Robertson Work has masterfully articulated a global vision so fundamental and practical that every citizen of Earth will applaud and hope for this future. Through his superb analysis of societal obstacles, broad strategies, and countless realistic actions, the resulting focus on six arenas of transformation illuminates possibility in the midst of our current experience of institutional challenge and collapse. This is all combined with such an honest sharing of Work's own profound humanness that the reader is compelled to keep reading until the end."

- R. Bruce Williams, international facilitator and author of *More Than 50 Ways to Build Team Consensus* and *12 Roles of Facilitators for School Change*

"*A Compassionate Civilization* is a surprisingly captivating and interesting book, which helps us delve into our roles in the past, present, and future. It is brilliantly stimulating and packed with thrilling images of human/planet history and its journey into the future. This book deserves to be hugely influential and readable for all who care for the future of Mother Earth."

- Tatwa P. Timsina, PhD, professor, author, and founder of ICA Nepal; former president of ICA International

This book is dedicated to my creative and caring grandchildren, Phoenix and Mariela, and all children around this beautiful planet. May they and all beings everywhere live in a compassionate civilization on a sustainable planet.

CONTENTS

ACKNOWLEDGMENTS

There are many people whom I would like to acknowledge and thank for their influence on my thinking, writing, and work. One of the earliest was Pierre Teilhard de Chardin, the French theologian-paleontologist whose books and life inspired me to advance the noosphere, the envelope of consciousness around our planet, and participate in cosmogenesis, the unfolding evolution of the universe. Joseph Wesley Mathews, dean of the Ecumenical Institute and Institute of Cultural Affairs (ICA), called me to serve the least, the last, and the lost and taught me effective methods and models of human development. Dr. Jean Houston, author and teacher extraordinaire, showed me how to release human capacities and engage in social artistry. Ken Wilber, philosopher, opened me to the power of integral systems thinking. Dr. G. Shabbir Cheema, director of governance programs at the East-West Center, welcomed me to the world of urban development at the United Nations Development Programme (UNDP) and invited me to consult for the East-West Center. Dr. Paul Smoke, professor of decentralization at NYU Wagner Graduate School of Public Service, invited me to design a course on innovative leadership for human development and to teach at NYU Wagner. Dr. Adriana Alberti, public administration senior advisor for the UN Department of Social and Economic Affairs/ Division of Public Administration and Development Management (UNDESA/DPADM), invited me to speak at several UN conferences. Dr. Tatwa Timsina, professor and founder of ICA Nepal, invited me to keynote the global human development conference in Kathmandu, Nepal. Joy Jinks, community organizer and author, invited me to speak at the Building Creative Communities Conference. Dr. Mark Davies, professor at Oklahoma City University and director of the World House, invited me to present at a creative peace-building symposium. Dr. Terry Bergdall, former ICA USA executive director, invited me to speak to a think tank on international development in Chicago. Karen Johnson, teacher at Horace Mann School in NYC, invited me to make a presentation to faculty, parents, and students. Dr. Juliet Chieuw and Jan Sanders invited me to speak at the University of Aruba. Lowie Kawasaki invited me to consult for UN Habitat in Nairobi. Bruce Williams, friend and author, encouraged me to publish this book. His Holiness the Fourteenth Dalai Lama is showing me how to live a compassionate and wise life. The Venerable Thich Nhat Hanh is teaching me to breathe in and out in awareness and gratitude. The late Gelek Rimpoche, Dr. Larry Ward and Dr.Peggy Rowe, have been my primary Buddhist teachers. Jeremy Rifkin, author of *The Empathic Civilization*, inspired me to write this book. Dr. Martin Luther King Jr. challenged me by his commitment to truth and justice for all. Mahatma Gandhi taught me about nonviolence as a philosophy and a way of changing society. My late wife, Mary Elizabeth Avery Work, journeyed with me in world service for thirty-five years. My mother and father, Mary and Robbie Work, always trusted my decisions. James Duncan Work, my brother, demonstrated the efficacy of meditation, vegetarianism, home schooling, and social media. Finally, my wife, Rev. Bonnie Myotai Treace, has stood by me with encouragement, wisdom, and love these past ten years, repeatedly urged me to publish this book, and inspires me to be the best person I can be. Deep gratitude to each of the above along with many others.

PREFACE

This book is being published now because of the urgent need for a compelling vision, practical actions, and effective tools to catalyze what has become necessary in this moment of multiple crises. It is offered as an opportunity to reflect deeply on what is happening in our communities and societies and how we can each help create a better world for all. In this book, you can participate in a conversation about this most critical decade and century. My heartfelt hope is that by dialoguing with these reflections, you might be challenged, inspired, and equipped to participate further in the adventure of realizing a compassionate civilization day by day.

I invite you to reflect on my analyses and recommendations related to our current systemic crises, the idea that a civilization of compassion is emerging at this very moment, and six arenas of transformation. We will also explore the "movement of movements" and the innovative leadership approaches that will get us to where we need to be. Finally, the book outlines the underlying self-understanding of global-local citizenship that is required and ends with over a quarter of the book devoted to a few trustworthy practices of care for self and others for those who would undertake this transformative work.

This book aims to serve the growing number of activists and caring citizens in the United States and around the world who know that *these are the times and we are the people*. It is not a technical book for experts; it is for everyone who cares. This is the moment for this book to be in your hands.

Most of these reflections were written between 2013 and 2015, each one an inspiration. After this creative period came to a natural conclusion, I organized the reflections into parts, chapters and subchapters.

Over the past seven years, I have given several speeches about these topics at four UN global forums on public service, a global human development conference, a nonprofit think tank, a university peace symposium, an elite high school, a community development conference, and classes at NYU Wagner. These took place in Dar es Salaam, Tanzania; Kathmandu, Nepal; Manama, Bahrain; Seoul, Republic of Korea; New York, New York; Chicago, Illinois; Oklahoma City, Oklahoma; and Colquitt, Georgia. For the past four years, I have written the blog *A Compassionate Civilization* to a worldwide readership about principles of sustainability, equality, justice, participation, tolerance, and nonviolence. In addition to speeches and blog posts, this book also contains some of my poetry and autobiographical material as a way to ground macroreflections in personal stories and images. I became convinced to share these thoughts in book form to encourage and assist those who care in their own thinking and action.

Even though I wrote this book before the November 2016 US presidential election, I have been well aware for several years of the national and global trends of oligarchy, misogyny, systemic poverty, racism, intolerance, and violence and the necessity to resist, persist, insist, and enlist. This book is not in the first instance about the US political landscape in 2017; however, it may provide some relief for the sadness and despair some citizens and activists feel concerning the present environment and generate new inspiration, energy, perspective, and action. This book is about lifelong commitment to social transformation. As author Naomi Klein says in her new book by the same name, "*No is not enough.*" We must dream a new world and create it through our own efforts.

My social and historical perspective is a product of three phases of professional engagement. First, for twenty-one years I was national or regional director of a nonprofit, the Institute of Cultural Affairs (ICA), conducting community, organizational, and leadership development projects and programs in Chicago, Malaysia, the Republic of Korea, Dallas, Jamaica, and Venezuela. Next, I worked for sixteen years with the United Nations Development Programme (UNDP) in New York City as principal policy advisor of decentralized governance assisting developing countries around the world in formulating policies and programs in local governance, urban development, and decentralization. Third, for the past ten years, I have been teaching innovative leadership and strategic management at New York University (NYU) Wagner Graduate School of Public Service in NYC, as well as consulting for the UN and the Fulbright Specialist Program and advising Trusted Sharing, a social media start-up. Therefore, because of this journey, my perspective on sustainable human development includes grassroots projects, national and global policies, and individual capacity development. Since most of my work has been in developing nations, it is only in the past few years that I have been engaged as an activist in my own country. In the past nine years, I have, among other activities, knocked on doors to get out the vote, called my representatives, written on social media, signed petitions, joined the local party precinct, and attended Our Revolution meetings.

HOW TO READ THIS BOOK. It is recommended that you begin at the beginning and read the parts, chapters, subchapters and reflections sequentially for the unfolding logic. The first half of the book is more about the *why* and *what* of a compassionate civilization, whereas the second half deals with the *how* and *who*. Or you can dive in and out of chapters, subchapters, or individual reflections that are of particular interest or importance to you. The table of contents gives you the major themes and the index gives you alphabetized reflection titles.

My intention for this book is that if it is anything it is a "multilogue," a conversation among many people—between you, me, and everyone else. I will write something, and you will reflect on some aspect of it and then offer your own thoughts, words, and deeds. Of course, others and I would love to know what you are thinking, and in fact it could help us a lot. But what is most important is that you have them and are them. In the same way, my written words are the result of my reflections on things I have experienced and thought. We are all in this together—a history-long, worldwide journey of consciousness.

The tone of this book will usually be informal and nonacademic, although there will sometimes be references to other sources.

After you read a reflection, subchapter, or chapter, I would invite you to respond to four questions (from the ICA's ORID conversation method):

Objective: What words, ideas, or images struck me?
Reflective: How did they make me feel, and what did they lead me to recall?
Interpretive: What is the significance or meaning of this for me?
Decisional: What do I decide to do in relation to this?

To post brief comments or questions about the book and to learn about what else is happening, please go to the Facebook page for *A Compassionate Civilization*: www.facebook.com/compassionatecivilization/

To participate in a longer, more in-depth discussion about the contents and implications of each chapter of this book, go to the Trusted Sharing online site, and join the global conversation concerning *A Compassionate Civilization* at www.trustedsharing.com/Robertson/1727

Enjoy the journey!

18 July 2017

PROLOGUE

As we begin, let us remind ourselves who we are as human beings, what constitutes a human society, and how far we have come as a civilization.

First, a bit of social philosophy. What is a *human* being? What is development? What then is human development? What is the purpose of societal organization and governance in relation to human development?

These are not only philosophical questions but also urgent, practical questions. These are some of the profound questions facing us as a species. Our responses to these questions, both in our individual thoughts and behaviors and in our collective cultures and systems, will determine how human society and life itself flourishes or declines on planet Earth. If this is so, how is it so?

There are many views of what constitutes a human being. Is a human being a spiritual being of infinite worth? Or primarily a consumer of goods and services? Or a resource for economic production? Or primarily a citizen of the state? Or simply another mammal? Or a child of God? Is a human being basically good? Or fundamentally evil? Does each human being who is born have universal rights guaranteed by society? What are the rights of future generations? What is the full potential of each human being? What is the ultimate purpose of human beings on planet Earth or in the universe as a whole? Our answers to these questions often arise from our own acculturation and socialization as provided by our culture, religion, political ideology, personal reflection, age, sex, and so forth. Some people believe that only their group is truly human and that all others lack truth and legitimacy.

The dominant answer in the world today to the question of what constitutes development is material and economic progress, industrialization, and modernization. The race is on to increase GDP per capita and fuel a consumption-production society at any cost to nature and people. However, this purely economic definition is doing much harm to natural systems and human culture.

Each definition of humanness carries with it an implicit or explicit definition of development. If a human being is primarily a spiritual being, then society should be designed in a way that would help each person realize his or her spiritual potential. If a human being is primarily a consumer, then he is to be manipulated by advertisements to purchase certain goods and services. If a human being is primarily a citizen of a democratic state, then she is empowered to express her opinions through voting and is responsible to act in accord with the laws of the state. If a human being is understood simply as another mammal, then he will be treated that way. If a human being is understood to be a child of God, then she will be cherished as a holy being.

If a human being is understood to be basically good, then a society would structure itself to nurture this quality and design systems based on trust of this basic goodness. If a human being is understood as fundamentally evil, then society will design systems that seek to control and punish these dark impulses. If every human being who is born has universal human rights, then society will design systems to ensure adequate opportunities and access to quality education, health care, housing, credit, and self-expression of each and every person. If future generations have the same rights as the present generation, then society will ensure that the resources of Earth are preserved and developed with this in mind. If every human being has the right to realize his or her full potential in this life, then society will be designed to ensure that this can happen. If human beings believe that they have an ultimate purpose on planet Earth and in the universe as a whole, then this will provoke profound dialogue in society and help direct the design of social systems toward a learning society.

What then is "human development"? As we have seen, different definitions will flow from different views of the human being. In the view of the United Nations and the international community, the human being is guaranteed universal rights by society as articulated in the Universal Declaration of Human Rights. The UN has been analyzing and promoting "human development" or "sustainable human development" over the past twenty years. Furthermore, the UN Millennium Development Goals (MDGs) and now the Sustainable Development Goals (SDGs) were agreed upon by member states to provide tangible targets for human development by 2030 (see the annex).

How then do nations and local communities understand the *social contract* that guides the design of social systems for the benefit of all human beings; all living beings; and the finite resources of planet Earth, including plants, animals, water, soil, and air? Based on the

Universal Declaration of Human Rights, the social contract includes that human beings agree to care for each other to ensure that each person has the necessary conditions for a full and meaningful life while ensuring that future generations have the same right.

This means that for all people to enjoy these rights, no group of individuals should be allowed to make this impossible by the overaccumulation of economic wealth, political power, or cultural dominance.

•   •   •

What is our journey to now and beyond? What has brought us to this moment? Scientists tell us that around fourteen billion years ago there was a great flaring forth of time, space, and energy coalescing in atoms and light and evolving into galaxies and stars, then into planets, and finally into plants and animals. And here we are today on our gorgeous planet Earth. What will be going on in another fourteen billion years?

Historians tell us that there are around five thousand years of recorded history. What do you hope will be going on in another five thousand years?

The industrial age began around 250 years ago. What do you hope could be happening in another 250 years?

With these reflections and questions as a backdrop, what are the current challenges facing humanity and, indeed, all life on Earth? Thus we begin to respond to this question in the first chapter.

PART 1

WHAT IS A COMPASSIONATE CIVILIZATION, AND WHY IS IT URGENT?

CHAPTER 1

OUR TIME OF CRISIS AND OPPORTUNITY

We are living in the most critical time in all of human history, a time to do what is needful or face the direst of consequences. Why do I say that? Never before in the past five thousand years have we faced such colossal dangers and such exhilarating possibilities. The very future of life on Earth is at stake. We face multiple, interlocking crises, any one of which could be decisive—climate chaos, misogyny, systemic poverty, oligarchy, prejudice, and a culture of violence. A whole system transformation is underway, and we are at the brink of either mass extinction or a whole new way of being human on planet Earth. Which it will be depends on what you and I do with our lives.

Climate Chaos and Degradation of Ecosystems

The natural systems of Earth that have supported human civilization for the past twelve thousand years are changing drastically, and human societies must change quickly, as well as adapt to an already-different Earth over the long term. The effects of global climate change and degradation of ecosystems are upon us. We had thought that fossil fuels were a brilliant solution for our energy needs. It turns out that they have been destroying our life support systems of air, water, ice, soil, plants, and animals by releasing carbon dioxide from the extraction and burning of coal, oil, and gas, creating "death energy"—energy derived from dead life forms that is killing living beings now. Carbon dioxide, methane gas, and other greenhouse gases released into the atmosphere are rapidly warming the planet. The Greenland ice cap is melting. Antarctica, which boasts 90 percent of Earth's ice, is melting. Mountain glaciers in the Andes and Himalayas and the Siberian permafrost are melting. We are at four hundred parts per million (ppm) of carbon dioxide in the atmosphere, already above 350 ppm, which has been calculated as the highest concentration possible without dangerously heating up Earth.

If the rise of carbon dioxide and the warmth of Earth's atmosphere go unabated, the oceans will rise up to six feet, flood coastal cities, and submerge many island nations and other inhabited landmasses. We already see acidification of the oceans, extensive deforestation, massive desertification, droughts, wildfires, and food collapse. Megastorms will become the norm. There is already a massive dieback of species, the sixth mass extinction (the first five: Ordovician-Silurian, Late Devonian, Permian, Triassic-Jurassic, and Cretaceous-Tertiary). There will be social, political, and economic volatility with mass migrations and resource wars. Drinking water will become scarce, and wars will be fought over this life-essential resource. The next several years will tell the story of our future—misery or happiness. I remind you of this not to frighten you but to sound the alarm that we must and can change our ways right now.

Patriarchy and Misogyny

For thousands of years, it has been understood that men are dominant and should control and lead women and society as a whole. This view is called *patriarchy* and has been strengthened by the world's religions with their predominately male gods, male saviors, and male priests. Some men fear and even hate women. Women have often been kept silent, subservient, abused, trapped at home, and pregnant and have not been allowed to exercise their human rights of speech, choice, career, and leadership. This is called *misogyny*.

The problem with these views is that in addition to harming women themselves, they have kept women from exercising their rightful leadership in society at all levels. Without honoring women's views, knowledge, and wisdom, societies have become overly masculinized and promote and celebrate violence and warfare, destruction of the natural world, harmful competition, and technology without heart.

Systemic Poverty and Social Deprivation

Two and a half billion people live on less than two dollars per day, and 2.6 billion lack access to sanitation. One billion have no access to safe water. Ten million preventable child deaths occur each year. In the past thirty years, income inequality has skyrocketed. One percent of the world's population owns 50 percent of the world's wealth. And in the United States, the top 1 percent owns as much wealth as the bottom 90 percent. We humans are still plagued by illiteracy, illness, and ignorance. Our educational systems are not adequate for all the people. Likewise, our health systems are tragically unable to provide even basic care to all people everywhere, and people suffer senseless illnesses.

Our modern economies are based on capital, profit, debt, interest, and the global gambling casino of investing. Money accumulation for a few has become more important than the well-being of all people and nature. Economic enterprises based on fossil fuel energy pollute the air, water, and soil and abuse human labor. Our economies are often killing us, other life-forms, and our planetary ecosystems. Fiscal policy is made by global elites that control the formation and movement of capital through central banks and investment firms. The 1 percent has become consumed by greed and power. Austerity for the masses and opulence for the few is not the human way.

The number of poor people has expanded, and the middle class has been significantly weakened. Many people don't have adequate income or access to quality education and health services. This is because the economic system based on accumulation and greed is designed to favor the wealthy. If you have money, you can make money with money. If you don't have money, you have to work for wages that are often inadequate to support you and your family. One of the many problems with this situation is that the majority of people are suffering and do not see how they can sustain their lives.

Oligarchy, Plutocracy, and Corporatocracy

The democratic experiment of more than three hundred years is faltering badly around the world. Oligarchy, plutocracy, and corporatocracy are masquerading as democratic regimes. Elites are manipulating democratic institutions to maintain control of political, economic, and military power. We are experiencing a deep crisis of governance. Democratic elections and representation around the world have been greatly weakened by a few powerful people. For example, only 158 families provided half of the money supporting presidential candidates for the 2016 US elections. When a few families control a country, it is called an *oligarchy*. When a few wealthy people control a country, it is called a *plutocracy*. In the United States and other nations, corporations are controlling elections, legislation, and the mass media as a way to control society. This is called *corporatocracy*. One of the problems with this trend is that the needs, voices, and wisdom of middle-class and poor people are being ignored, and they are suffering.

Bigotry and Prejudice

People who are different or in the minority are often looked down on and frequently harmed. This includes people of different races, ethnic groups, religions, economic classes, and sexual orientations. People often fear and hate others who exhibit different beliefs, cultural norms, and personal behaviors. We face a crisis of the "sunset effect"—that is, when an era is ending, there is often the brief appearance of its strengthening, as in the last burst of a sunset's rays. We see this effect in fear-based religious fundamentalisms that are at war with an empirical, scientific worldview and the principles of inclusiveness and respect for differences of opinion. This, of course, is called *bigotry* or *prejudice*.

These confused views are based on ignorance and misunderstanding of the basic rights of every person and group to be who and what they decide. Many people are not aware that there are not many races but rather only one human race. The problem with these views is that they cause many people to suffer.

Continuous Warfare and a Culture of Violence

There are enough nuclear weapons on Earth to destroy human civilization several times over. Some countries shoot missiles into other countries without being attacked or provoked and without UN authorization. Some conflicts rage on for decades, destroying infrastructure and human communities and creating huge numbers of refugees seeking safety and new homes. People in other countries are often feared and attacked with massive use of armaments. This is *militarism*. People think that their country is always right and is the only one that is important. This is called *nationalism*.

Many people assume that a pervasive culture of violence is natural and inevitable. Entertainment, media, and video games extend violence into the everyday life of adults and children. The value and meaning of human life is demeaned or denied in all of this.

• • •

These six crises are interwoven and mutually causative. There is, however, a doorway and a pathway forward. The crises themselves are actually opportunities that can wake us up to our delusions and self-inflicted suffering and motivate us to reinvent our societies. In the next chapter, we explore the visions, obstacles, strategies, and actions that can carry us toward our greatest potential as humans.

CHAPTER 2

AN EMERGING CIVILIZATION OF COMPASSION: VISION, OBSTACLES, STRATEGIES, AND ACTIONS

The Big Picture

What then is the big picture, the overarching narrative of our times? Is it inevitable that we are moving through a time of systems collapse, suffering, and death? Or could something else be emerging? What if the breaking down of our unsustainable, unjust, authoritarian, unequal, and divisive systems is forcing us to reinvent these systems based on healthy and hopeful principles of sustainability, justice, participation, equality, and inclusiveness? What if these crises are really opportunities to redesign our societies as part of a new, empathic civilization of sustainable human development that works for everyone?

Our current systems are not working for the human population or for other life-forms. Ours is a time of crisis that can wake us from this nightmare so that we can create a new way of being, a way of well-being for and on this Earth. Empathy has always been a deep part of the human psyche and is now being called by necessity, for survival's sake, to emerge as the driving force for a new civilization of mutuality and care. Every day, it is proved again and again that people care about each other, including those who are far away and from different nations, cultures, religions, and races. Human beings are fundamentally empathic because we are deeply interconnected with one another and recognize ourselves in each other. We each want happiness and health. We feel each other's suffering and joy. We are a big family of brothers and sisters, which includes other life-forms as well. More than seven billion human beings are present on this Earth today with our unique intelligence, creativity, compassion, and understanding to take us through this dangerous transition. This is the moment of citizens to the rescue.

The new civilization will be based on a social contract of the interdependence of people with each other and with natural systems. The renewable energy of sun, wind, and water will sustain our social and economic life. The protection of natural systems of soil, water, plants, and animals will be embodied in both collective law and individual behavior. Governance systems will be based on the needs and voice of all the people, not just the economic, political, and cultural elites. Accountability, transparency, and responsiveness will be present at all levels of government.

Fiscal systems will be designed to provide equity to all people. Global and local economies will be concerned about the rights and well-being of workers and the environment. Health care and education will be universal rights in policy and practice. Cultural diversity will flourish, and people will delight in their differences and enjoy learning from each other's knowledge and wisdom. Consumption and production will be replaced as the highest good of society by mutual learning, care, artistic expression, and other forms of creativity.

This new civilization will be the flowering of the planetary and human project. Is this a vision of utopia? I would submit that we have a radical choice to make—to move toward either a sustainable and humanizing world or a world of endless dystopia of chaos and suffering.

Emergence

Each of the crises identified in the previous chapter is an unparalleled opportunity for reinventing our societies. We have the tools and technology needed to solve each of these crises, but we lack the collective agreement and will to take action. We must, at the same time, transform individual consciousness and behavior and collective cultures and systems. These crises are an opportunity to reinvent nothing less than human society itself from the bottom up and the top down based on principles of sustainability, equality, justice, participation, tolerance, and nonviolence. We can literally create, moment by moment, a world that works for everyone—societies that enable each person to realize her or his full potential.

Within this very moment of crisis, a new civilization is emerging. It is an Earth-based civilization of sustainable human development. In this new civilization, people will embody a consciousness of being part of the living Earth, of being part of the life force of our beautiful planet. We are all earthlings. All people and all life-forms are our brothers and sisters. We have a common future or no future at all. People will exhibit behavior that is empathic and compassionate. People will manifest a culture of peace, creativity, and learning. People will create systems, policies, and institutions of sustainability and justice.

Toward a Compassionate Civilization

Compassion is not to pity but to suffer with, to understand, to empathize, to feel, to be with and for. I am on your side. I am like you, and you are like me. We are one. We both suffer. We both desire happiness and the relief of suffering. I vow to help relieve your suffering. Compassion.

Civilization is civil, civility, about the citizen, the one who belongs. It has many dimensions—cultural, social, political, economic, and environmental. What if everyone were to belong to this emerging civilization, all people and all life-forms—an Earth community, the biosphere, the noosphere (the layer of consciousness enveloping our planet), human society as part of great nature?

Even now, a compassionate civilization is emerging. We have come thus far over these billions, millions, thousands, hundreds of years. Will we yet go further, further than ever before? Will we, you and I, embrace all, everyone, as a sister and fellow citizen of Earth society? Will we suffer together? Relieve our suffering together? Laugh together? Be happy together? Realize our full potential together? It is possible, you know. And it has become an utter necessity. Will we make it together or not make it at all?

The choice is ours. Would we not rather angle toward a compassionate civilization? Let's go together.

How would we design such a civilization? How would we construct it? How would we embody it in our minds, behaviors, cultures, and systems?

Let's explore together. In fact, many are already at work on this great and noble task. Many individuals of goodwill and their organizations, networks, and movements are hard at work around the planet. Let's recognize each other, thank each other, encourage each other, and move forward together. Some are at work on climate chaos mitigation and adaptation, renewable energy, and sustainable environment. Others are promoting gender equality and human rights. And still others are working for social and economic justice, cultural and religious tolerance, participatory and transparent governance, peace and nuclear disarmament, and spiritual practice and enlightenment.

Yes, of course there is resistance. There are powerful forces saying that it is impossible to construct a compassionate civilization. They will resist, block, and fight. They will say that human beings are weak and selfish and must be controlled and punished. The powerful will say that they deserve their power and will try to maintain a civilization of inequality, injustice, unsustainability, nonparticipation, intolerance, and violence. They will use force to get their way. But the more than seven billion of us humans and countless billions of other life-forms will move forward like an unstoppable tidal wave, droplet by gentle droplet. The stakes are too high not to press on.

People and Planet

Why the name "compassionate civilization"?

I was very pleased when Jeremy Rifkin published in 2009 his groundbreaking book, *The Empathic Civilization*. Contrary to the belief that human beings are basically selfish, he clearly shows that human beings are fundamentally empathic. We are programmed to feel what others feel.

When I imagined a world of sustainable human development catalyzed by a movement of movements, I began to use the term *empathic civilization*. Over the past few years, I wrote and spoke about this vision in UN global conferences and in my graduate classes at NYU Wagner: "Ours is a critical decade and century of crisis and opportunity. We *can* create a new, empathic civilization. We can and must mitigate climate chaos, protect the environment, achieve gender equality, promote social and economic justice, institutionalize participatory governance, and realize cultural tolerance."

After working with this for some time, I came to understand that we must move beyond empathy to build a *compassionate* civilization. What is the difference? With empathy, we feel what others are feeling and identify with them. Compassion goes further by sharing in the suffering of others and vowing to relieve their suffering. We suffer together, and we will relieve our suffering together. My own experience confirms what all the world's wisdom traditions have articulated—that compassion and understanding are the deep structures of being human.

For me, combining compassion and civilization provides an inspiring vision of a macro-historical-societal system infused with a powerful ethical stance based in human nature itself. My hope is that this concept may empower those of us working to create a better world, a world that works for everyone and protects the environment, and one that is both pro-people and pro-planet.

May we relieve the suffering of all beings everywhere.

A Practical Vision

Reflecting on Today, Yesterday, and Tomorrow

Today, we celebrate the victory before the victory. We celebrate the emergence of a new civilization of compassion. It is even now in our midst. It is often hard to see, given the chaos and suffering surrounding us and filling our minds. Yet we see it again and again in the many simple acts of kindness between and among people.

Earlier, I shared a few thoughts about a compassionate civilization just to get things started. Before sharing a few concrete images of a vision of a new civilization of compassion, I should first say something about the nature of visioning.

I agree with the statement "Where there is no vision, the people perish" (Proverbs 29). Having a sense of where you are going—or, more importantly, where you want to go—is very important to human motivation and happiness. If we are cut off from a sense of a meaningful future, it is often hard to live in this moment. However, the good news is that this moment is full and perfect and contains memories, anticipations, and the gift of the "eternal now."

The more visceral and experiential our vision is of a hoped-for future, the more motivation we have to move toward it. It is what Dr. Jean Houston calls the "lure of becoming." We are literally pulled toward an attractive image and vision of a future that we desire. When we begin to envision a new civilization of kindness and happiness, we must do so on many levels and dimensions. We will experience this vision with our five senses, with our mind's eye, through stories and symbols, and with a profound sense of embodiment. We will also envision a hoped-for future in terms of the new mind-sets, behaviors, cultures, and systems that will comprise it. But we won't begin that process just yet.

Imagining a Hoped-for Civilization of Compassion

Yes, we need to be clear on the crises, problems, and challenges, but we also need to dream of a new world that is so attractive that it beckons us and motivates us to create it. What are your greatest hopes for the future? What is indeed possible? What is necessary? What would a new civilization of compassion look like? Remember, compassion is not only feeling the pain of others but also vowing to relieve others' suffering.

Compassion in the first instance is not religious or even spiritual. It is a natural response of living beings who have empathy for each other and want to help each other. Parents are one of the best examples of compassion. They will do anything to help relieve the suffering of their children and to help them be happy. A compassionate civilization is the universalization of this quality of compassion directed toward all beings everywhere. Or it can be called love, or care, or being neighborly, or helpful.

What might a new civilization of compassion look like? It will be based on six principles: sustainability, equality, justice, participation, tolerance, and nonviolence.

Environmental Sustainability

The new civilization of compassion will embody environmental sustainability at its very core. As Naomi Klein writes, "Climate change isn't just a crisis. It's a chance to build a better world." We will protect the natural environment. People will realize that there can be no human life without healthy ecosystems of air, water, soil, plants, and animals. We will keep the remaining fossil fuels—death energy—in the ground. All energy will be from renewable sources, such as the sun, wind, water, geothermal sources, and algae—or "life energy." The new economy will be 100 percent environmentally friendly. The green revolution will sustain life on Earth for millions of years.

Gender Equality

A compassionate civilization will embody gender equality in every facet of human society. Women will be leaders at every level of society. They will be paid the same as men for the same work. The voices, views, and wisdom of women will be honored and celebrated. Men will respect and protect the sovereignty of women's bodies and minds. Gender and sexual orientation will be understood and accepted as taking a multiplicity of forms. Women, who "hold up half the sky," will be free to be whom and what they are.

Socioeconomic Justice

A compassionate civilization will embody socioeconomic justice. Everyone will have meaningful engagement, adequate income, and access to high-quality education and health services as a human right. We will reinvent money as a means of caring for all life on Earth and stop the endless drive for profit, extraction, consumption, production, and wealth accumulation. We will learn "sacred economics" from Charles Eisenstein, with capital not being based on debt and interest. Bartering will increase. Local currencies will be developed. We will create local, national, and global economies that are pro-people and pro-planet. We will make the shift from an economy based on greed to an economy of generosity.

Participatory Governance

A compassionate civilization will embody participatory governance to achieve the UN's Sustainable Development Goals (SDGs). The needs, voices, views, and wisdom of all people will set the policy agendas for society through new processes and institutions of direct democracy. This will include face-to-face and online policy dialogue. Accountability, transparency, and responsiveness will be present at all levels of governance. E-governance will bring policy-making closer to the people.

Cultural Tolerance

A compassionate civilization will embody cultural tolerance. It will be understood and accepted that all people of every race, ethnic background, religion, economic class, lifestyle orientation, and nationality will be respected and free to exercise their rights as human beings. People will enjoy learning from others who have different backgrounds and orientations to life. Empathic consciousness will be the new common sense. An evolutionary Earth story will be understood by all.

Peace and Nonviolence

A compassionate civilization will embody peace and nonviolence. There will be no nuclear weapons. War itself will be seen as illegitimate. A culture of peace will prevail as everyone comes to understand empathy and compassion as the underlying foundations of being human.

• • •

At this point, you may again be saying to yourself, "But all this sounds utopian. Is it really possible to achieve?" I would say again to you that if we do not head for utopia, we will be left in endless dystopia of environmental degradation and social misery. Let's go for it!

The following are further individual reflections from recent years, concerning a practical vision of a compassionate civilization.

What Are You Really Doing?

Today, the UN General Assembly opens. Manhattan will be in gridlock. I am reminded of my many days working across the street at the UNDP as a policy advisor. Today, I am a teacher and consultant. How can I make a difference globally and locally? How can my actions help hasten the arrival of a compassionate civilization? When terrorists attack a mall in Nairobi, killing innocent people, how can I respond compassionately, both to the tragedy of Somalia and to the victims? How can I help stop the fossil fuel industry, child trafficking, the abuse of women, or corporate greed? How can my meager words and deeds relieve such vast suffering?

We are bombarded daily by crisis and tragedy. First, it was the Westgate Mall in Nairobi. A few months before that, it was Hurricane Sandy. Tomorrow, we can count on being confronted by something else.

How might it be helpful to envision a compassionate civilization manifesting in some future time when we face so many crises today and need to act on so many fronts? I believe that we need both—a compelling vision of a long-term systems transformation and our concrete work in the day to day. A long-term vision can inspire us with hope and direction while our daily efforts inspire us with a sense of relevance and accomplishment.

Most change agents are focused on a single issue. If we have a civilizational vision, we can feel ourselves being part of a massive movement of movements, moving relentlessly toward our most cherished hopes and dreams. By identifying an emerging civilization based on principles of compassion, sustainability, equality, justice, participation, and tolerance, we can sense our individual contributions as part of something larger and more profound. We are not only mitigating climate change, we are catalyzing a whole system shift resulting in a compassionate civilization.

I am reminded of the old story of the stonecutters in the Middle Ages of Europe. Someone asked one stonecutter what he was doing. He said, "I am cutting stones." The person asked another stonecutter the same question. He replied, "I am supporting my family." Then, the person asked yet another stonecutter, who said with dignity and passion, "I am building a cathedral!" Was each stonecutter doing the same thing? What difference does your vision make in your day-to-day life?

———

What Does Compassion Smell Like?

We know that there is only change. We look back at history and evolution and should be astounded by the radical transformations that have brought us to this moment—from clans of hunter-gatherers to farming settlements, to cities and empires, to a single planetary ecology. And we are all visionaries. Our visions are hopeful, despairing, or boring. How we use our imaginations, not just our intellects, is a powerful force in creating the future. If we are indeed able to avoid dystopia, what are our best hopes and dreams for the future of life on Earth? What might a compassionate civilization look, sound, feel, taste, and smell like?

When I walk around in a hoped-for future, I see smiles, hear laughter, feel warmth, taste gratitude, and smell possibility. I see art everywhere and groups of people sharing ideas and stories. I hear someone acknowledging a challenging experience a stranger is having in a way that honors that stranger. People stop to tell me that they feel happy to be alive. People are enjoying the fascinating tastes of healthy foods from different cultures. I smell really, really fresh air.

I see the headline "CEOs Agree Tenfold Is Fair" marking a new policy that a company's highest salary will be no more than ten times that of the lowest. I hear people talking with each other about their observations, art practices, crafts, gardens, reflections, poetry, inventions, commitments, and spiritual practices. People feel at ease with others from very different backgrounds and lifestyles. People taste oneness and smell compassion.

What about you? When you close your eyes and visualize a hoped-for future, what pops up? What is going on in your new compassionate culture, family structure, economy, political process, health system, educational structure, and ecosystem? Enjoy the image, and then let the warmth of your vision flow into your life and work.

———

Four Faces of the Future

Using the framework of Ken Wilber's four integral systems quadrants (interior/exterior and individual/collective), what will be the new mind-sets, behaviors, cultures, and systems of the emerging civilization of compassion?

Four-Quadrant Integral Framework (Ken Wilber)		
	Interior	**Exterior**
Individual	- Mind-set - Consciousness - Awareness - Values - Attitudes	- Behavior - Interpersonal - Group Skills - Relationships - Partnerships
Collective	- Culture - Myth/Stories - Rituals - Symbols - Norms	- Systems - Organizations - Institutions - Communities - Policies

To get us started, I will share a few vision elements, and then it is your turn.

Individual Mind-sets

Individuals will exhibit a common sense of mutuality and interdependence. An awareness of our planet's fragile ecosystem will be widespread. Individuals will understand whole systems and think in integral patterns and processes. Intuition will be as important as rationality. Individuals will value integrity and kindness above all else. Education will have expanded people's understanding to include vast stretches of time and space. Individuals will grasp that they are each unique and unrepeatable and have special capacities to be developed and shared with others. People will think of themselves as citizens of the universe, the Milky Way galaxy, our solar system, and planet Earth.

Individual Behaviors

People will tend to act responsibly toward each other and the natural world. Leadership will have become servant leadership—facilitative, interactive, dialogical, participatory, profound, inspirational, and authentic. Teamwork and collaboration will be common practice. Individuals will be genuinely interested in other people of different mind-sets, lifestyles, cultures, and religions and desire to learn from them. People will gather in beautiful, green public spaces for social and political discourse and to share their insights, creativity, knowledge, and questions. Almost everyone will be engaged in spiritual practices such as meditation, contemplation, prayer, yoga, visualization, journal writing, or community celebrations.

Collective Cultures

Cultures will have evolved to assume sex and gender equality and human rights as the natural order of things. Equality and justice will be held as universal values. Care for natural systems of water, air, soil, plants, and animals will be deeply ingrained in the collective psyche. New stories and myths will have been fashioned from empirical observation and analysis of the evolution of the universe and life on Earth. There will be many powerful symbols of unity, compassion, and understanding. The historical religions will have evolved to honor each other's profound insights of reality, human nature, love, and truth. Many heroines and heroes who helped humanity realize a civilization of compassion will be celebrated widely. Happiness and well-being will be understood as the birthright of every living creature. Great celebrations of life on Earth will take place frequently.

Collective Systems

Renewable energy will be the law of the land, and climate change will have been mitigated. Governance institutions, policies, and systems will be highly responsive, accountable, and transparent to citizen participation and opinion by virtue of respectful face-to-face dialogue and consensus-building and through the Internet and social media. Education, health care, housing, water, food, and income will be universal rights, as will other basic necessities of life. Economies will be designed to provide needed goods and services for the well-being of all people and nature. Money will have been reinvented as an instrument for universal well-being rather than for individual power and control. The family will have evolved to embrace different possibilities for localized commitment, care, and nurture. The justice system would have shifted its orientation from judgment and punishment to accountability, reconciliation, and rehabilitation.

Yes, may it be so!

What stands out for you in the above? How does it make you feel? Based on these elements, what story would you tell about a compassionate civilization? When you consider what you have read, what are any implications for your life and work?

What are some of your own vision elements of a civilization of compassion? Please write them down and share with your friends, colleagues, or family members.

One of my questions is, how can I embody a future vision in my present life and work?

Breaking the Trance, Changing the Stance

In a compassionate civilization, empathy, altruism, and kindness will be preeminent values and expressions. Whole societies will greatly admire these qualities and the individuals and groups that manifest them. Greed will be seen as a base desire. Selfishness and harming others will be understood as tragic character flaws. Humility, sharing, cooperation, and collaboration will be celebrated as highly evolved traits.

It will be commonly understood that happiness is a way of being instead of a goal to be sought. Happiness will not be experienced in the acquisition of things but through helping others and being alive to daily relationships, observations, reflections, learning, creativity, and communication.

Entire societies of a compassionate civilization will exalt the common good and will ensure that both the natural and the built commons are sustained and sustainable while celebrating the unique contributions of individuals, communities, organizations, cultures, and bioregions. Societies will continually refine themselves to ensure that optimal conditions are in place for developing and sharing the full potential of each living being.

In a compassionate civilization, humanity has awakened from the trance of ever-increasing consumption-production and has evolved to never-ending learning-caring.

One resource that illustrates this vision beautifully is the profound Charter for Compassion movement launched by Karen Armstrong. There is a video at charterforcompassion.org of youth and adults speaking the inspiring words of the charter.

May we each realize happiness, peace, understanding, and compassion!

Dreams, Disappointments, Discontinuities

The future is both a continuation of and a departure from the past. On the one hand, there is nothing new under the sun. On the other, nothing is ever the same. There is only change. And what we do in the present moment can bend history or spark evolution in entirely new directions.

The flow of cause and effect, including DNA and cultural assumptions, maintains the repetition of old habits. Yet a new idea, word, deed, or technology can create a surprising new possibility. How can this be? How can these two forces inform those who would catalyze a compassionate civilization?

Earlier, we did a bit of dreaming of a new future of deep structural compassion and understanding. From today's perspective, it may seem utterly impossible to realize. However, when we look at transformations in evolution and history that have brought us to this moment, we are shocked by discontinuity after discontinuity.

For example, our species has journeyed from the advent of speech, to writing by hand, to the printing press, radio, telephone, television, the Internet, and now social media and artificial intelligence. Five thousand or even one hundred years ago, who would have believed that we could be blogging with anyone on planet Earth in real time?

Or, think of the ideas and social inventions that have changed human history. A short list could include the advent of tribal customs, ethics and law, the polis, conscience, universal love, common law, freedom, equality, democracy, the scientific method, human rights, evolution, and ecology.

Our dreams can become reality if we invest them with clarity and passion and commit ourselves to speak, write, invent, and embody them regardless of doubts, setbacks, and disappointments.

Yes, we *can and will* catalyze a compassionate civilization of climate change mitigation and adaptation…renewable energy…sovereignty and leadership of women at all levels of society…participatory and transparent governance…universal education and health care…economic opportunity and justice…cultural and religious tolerance…individual creativity and expression…and spiritual practice and development.

The movement of movements is alive and well.

———

I Dream a World

Imagination is very powerful. Architects imagine their creations before putting pen to paper. Drafters of constitutions imagine how their nations will function effectively. Athletes imagine achieving perfect form before competing. Visualizing, dreaming, and envisioning are practical tools for inventing the new. Each one of us imagines what we hope the future will bring. How might we imagine a new world of sustainable human development?

I dream a world of

- an abundance of safe water, food, and other life sustenance and a sharing of that abundance with all people and all life-forms;
- societies devoted to creating conditions that foster the discovery and realization of each person's full creativity, potential, and spiritual awakening;
- women in leadership roles at every level of society in equal partnership and mutual respect with men;

- ubiquitous music, art, poetry, dance, and theater performed and enjoyed by everyone who wishes;
- a universal love for learning about, reading about, and exploring mental landscapes;
- peace, harmony, and tranquility balanced with passion, challenge, and a zest for living fully;
- natural beauty of land, water, air, plants, and animals;
- architectural elegance of dwellings and the commons for all;
- 100 percent renewable energy from the sun, wind, water, geothermal sources, and biomass;
- sustainable local communities of significant, trusting, and happy relationships;
- planetary virtual conversation involving ten billion human minds and voices;
- meaningful celebrations of every individual birth, life milestone, and death and every societal, cultural, religious, and planetary milestone;
- physical, emotional, and mental health enjoyed by all;
- participatory decision-making in governance at local, national, regional, and planetary levels;
- lifelong education for all children and adults in the physical and social sciences and the arts and humanities;
- fiscal, monetary, and economic systems that promote the well-being of all people and all of nature;
- a rich diversity of lifestyles with mutual respect, understanding, and sharing of insights about being human;

- families devoted to the development of children and the care and happiness of each member;
- continuous innovation of safe technologies that will enhance the experience of being alive; and
- a vast number of optional and changing roles for living, working, serving, creating, and learning.

May we each awaken and live our dream. May our dreams indeed come true. May our dreams lead us, pull us, and push us ever onward with hope and passion. May the words *I have a dream* always resound in our hearts. May "dream time" be our time. May you have a good dream this day and this night, so that many others may wake up one fine day in a new reality.

• • •

Continuing with the strategic planning process developed by the Institute of Cultural Affairs, next we will begin to analyze the obstacles that could block the realization of a vision of a compassionate civilization (of which there are many). Then, we will identify the strategies that will deal with those blocks and move us toward our vision. Next, we will create action and implementation plans. In part 2 of this book, we will explore some of the effective methodologies and tools that we can learn and use.

———

Underlying Obstacles

What do you think are the biggest obstacles facing us? What is holding us back from realizing a compassionate civilization? What blocks, gaps, and inhibiting factors do we presently experience? They are legion, of course, and powerful and threatening. But after we identify them and their underlying root system, we may discover that they are the doorways to the future. But that is for later. Right now, let's take a look with unflinching honesty at some of our current obstacles.

Roadblocks

Using Wilber's quadrants of mind-sets, behaviors, cultures, and systems again, here is a quick brainstorm of current roadblocks:

Individual Mind-sets

"I'm all that matters. Climate change is a hoax. Women are men's property. Nature is an endless resource. Guns keep us safe. War is the way to resolve disputes. Animals don't have intelligence or feelings. Water is just a commodity. Austerity will strengthen the economy. The bottom line is money. If people can't make it on their own, they should die. My race is superior. Poor people are lazy. Only my religion is true. If someone does something wrong, that person should be locked away. We don't need government. Government is the problem. The UN is trying to take over the world. Evolution is not true. Science and learning are dangerous. Unlimited profit keeps the economy going. My language is superior. Greed is good. I am filled with hate. Narcissism is natural."

Individual Behaviors

"I must pack a gun. Rape is the woman's fault. Child abuse just happens. I have many addictions (TV, sex, drugs, overeating, etc.). Sometimes, my wife makes me hit her. Human beings are naturally violent. Sometimes, you have to be disrespectful and put people in their place. Bullying is part of being a kid. Lying is the way to get your way. If I get angry or am afraid, I will probably have to shoot someone."

Collective Cultures

"We believe in male dominance in government, business, family, etc. We champion the profit motive. The suit is our uniform. We value greed, wealth, and conspicuous consumption. We must consume more and produce more. We are destined to dominate nature. We believe that we will always have poor people. We believe that might makes right."

Collective Systems

"We extract, process, and burn fossil fuels. We remove mountain-tops. We pollute the air and water. We frack. We are increasing ocean acidification. We are causing megastorms, droughts, fires, deforestation, food-production collapse, glacial melting, sea rise, and the loss of coastal areas and islands. We promote GMOs and unhealthy food.

We have costly or unavailable health care. We have systemic poverty. We have nuclear power plants with radioactive waste. We must have dividends and interest to make money from money. We should have low taxation for the rich. We encourage unlimited incomes. We have crumbling infrastructure. We abuse and neglect the commons and public goods. We must govern ourselves through fascism, plutocracy, oligarchy, corporatocracy, systemic corruption, biased media, and cronyism."

———

Deep Roots of Confusion and Harm

What are the deep roots supporting and holding the aforementioned realities that are blocking the emergence of a compassionate civilization? Greed, pride, fear, anger, hatred, and ignorance are some of the deepest roots of confusion and harm.

Greed: the belief that one cannot have too much, even if others have little or nothing; the behavior of amassing more and more wealth and power and being unwilling to share with others; the culture of narcissism, conspicuous consumption, and materialism; the systems that allow a few individuals to make money with money without appropriate taxation for the maintenance of the commons, public goods, and assistance for those who are less fortunate.

Pride: the belief that my race, sex, culture, religion, and political ideology are superior to all others; the behavior of caring only for oneself and one's small circle; the culture of egoism, patriarchy, racism, sexism, ethnocentricity, xenophobia, theocracy, homophobia, and ideological rigidity; the systems that allow a few people to oppress others and force their views on them.

Fear: the belief that the self is in danger and that people who are different are dangerous; the behavior of armoring and arming oneself; the culture of insecurity, defensiveness, and protection; the systems that protect the wealthy and the powerful.

Anger: the belief that one's negative emotions toward others should be expressed; the behavior of doing harm to others with words and actions; the culture of violence; the systems of weapons and warfare.

Hatred: the belief that the other deserves to be despised; the behavior of harming others; the culture of violence; the systems that allow the other to be controlled and punished.

Ignorance: the belief that other people and nature are not as important as oneself; the behavior of doing harm to other people and ecosystems; the culture of total self-absorption; the systems that allow a few wealthy and powerful people to distort society toward their own gain without concern for others.

We must find and create many ways to awaken ourselves and others to authentic understanding and compassion. Remember: "The task before us now, if we would not perish, is to shake off our ancient prejudices, and to build the Earth" (Teilhard de Chardin, *Building the Earth*, page vii).

———

Example of an Obstacle: Outrageous Partisan Politics

Why am I so agitated by partisan politics that so often lead to the threat of shutdown of the federal government of my country? And what does it have to do with what is blocking our movement toward a compassionate civilization?

I know that there are people and organizations of tremendous wealth and religious and ideological fervor who believe that many, if not most, of the policies and programs of the federal government, and not simply the Affordable Care Act, are wrong and should be eliminated or changed. They feel justified in strangling the federal government and shutting off essential services to citizens. I feel, however, that this is outrageous and harmful and should not be allowed.

What do you think would happen if someone on the city council of New York even tried to shut down all city services? There would be outrage, and that person would be dismissed and held accountable. What do you think Exxon's shareholders, employees, and clients would do if someone on the board of directors tried to shut down the company? That director would be fired or voted out immediately.

Government is one of the three actors of governance, the other two being civil society and the private sector. Government is necessary for the orderly functioning of a society at every level—local; city;

state; national; and, increasingly, planetary. It maintains a framework of law, safety, and accountability.

It provides essential services of public health, education, communication, and transportation; regulations to ensure safe food, drugs, environmental conditions, and financial and investment transactions; diplomacy and national defense; a safety net for the elderly and the poor; a common currency; a forum for deliberation and consensus; a symbol of unity; and on and on.

How can it even be contemplated to shut down the federal government that holds fifty states and more than three hundred million people together as one community, provides essential services for citizens, and has obligations with countries around the world? Unthinkable.

A compassionate society is governed by the priorities of all its citizens to ensure their happiness and well-being and is committed to being a responsible and generous member of the world community.

———

Strategic Directions

A Perfect Storm

What is the responsible thing to do when you sense imminent danger? Should you make other people aware of it, even if you don't know what they should do? I think so. If you see a tornado forming, you should send out the alarm, even though you can't tell each person and family exactly what they should do.

Well, I sense that a perfect storm is brewing, involving not only climate chaos but political, economic, cultural, and social chaos as well. I wish it were not true. I hope that it doesn't happen. But I think that I have sighted a hurricane heading our way. Look out. Prepare. Act. Care for self and others.

Climate chaos is headed our way with megastorms, floods, droughts, and fires. The oceans are dying of rapid acidification. Ice caps and glaciers are melting and will flood coastlines and islands. Food production will be reduced. And so on. What to do? How to prepare? How to stop further environmental degradation and suffering? We know that we must stop burning fossil fuels. But will we? Just say yes.

Political chaos is headed our way with government shutdowns, unlimited campaign contributions, gerrymandering, and more filibusters. And so on. What to do? How to prepare? How to stop further degeneration of democratic institutions? We know that we must have government by, for, and of the people. But will we? Just say yes.

Economic chaos is headed our way with possible defaulting on the debt, possible currency devaluation, increased joblessness, and more toxic investments and bubbles. And so on. What to do? How to pre-pare? How to stop further collapse of the economic system? We know that we must have an economy that is fair and provides a living wage for all the people. But will we? Just say yes.

Cultural chaos is headed our way with increased fear, hysteria, and hatred of women and people of different races, religions, or sexual orientation. And so on. What to do? How to prepare? How to stop further deterioration of the fabric of trust and respect? We know that we must have a vibrant culture of dialogue and diversity. But will we? Just say yes.

Social chaos is headed our way with attacks on health care re-form and quality and affordable education for all our children and youth. And so on. What to do? How to prepare? How to stop further unraveling of our social fabric of care for all the people? We know that we must strengthen our social contract and ensure a decent and happy life for all the people. But will we? Just say yes.

What does *yes* look like? How do we speak, live, and do it?

There is a big difference between this perfect storm and a hur-ricane. In this case, we the people can affect many of the outcomes, whether for good or ill, whether short lived or long term. Yes, let's.

––––––––

Collapse, Goo, Butterfly!

As I write and speak about our time of whole systems transformation, it is dawning on me afresh that this entails a messy, challenging period of collapse; a time of gooeyness, redesign, and struggle; and then an energetic rebuilding phase. It's sort of like becoming a butterfly after caterpillar deconstruction and interim gooeyness and reorganization. We are in the first phase of collapse but need to be working on the design of a new societal order.

Are we headed toward a degraded planet ruled by the superrich and religious fundamentalists? Or are we going to create a new civilization based on compassion, sustainability, equality, justice, participation, and tolerance? What strategies are needed now and over the next two decades that will deal with what is blocking our movement toward our noble vision? Let's brainstorm a few strategies to get started.

Transforming Mind-sets and Values

- Universal education from preschool to university in the arts, humanities, social sciences, evolution, and other physical sciences
- Training in mindfulness practices, such as meditation, yoga, journaling, and community celebrations
- Training in compassion for and understanding of all people, air, water, land, animals, and plants
- Training in creative thinking regarding time, space, energy, patterns, models, relationships, societal systems, and Earth ecosystems

Changing Individual Behavior

- Training and modeling of group facilitation, integral development, and social artistry

- Training and modeling of team building, dialogue, collaboration, and cooperation
- Training and modeling of responsible behavior in relation to people and planet
- Training and modeling of nonviolence and peacemaking

Catalyzing Cultural Evolution

- Assuming a new common sense of sexual and gender equality and human rights
- Promoting a culture of compassion, understanding, happiness, and peace
- Manifesting a culture that celebrates learning and the realization of each person's full potential
- Creating science-based myths and stories of the evolution of the universe, the earth, life, and consciousness

Redesigning Whole Systems

- Designing policies and institutions that ensure sustainable ecosystems that protect the atmosphere, oceans, land, animals, plants, and humans
- Designing social policies and institutions of health care, education, protection, and justice for all
- Designing economic and fiscal policies and institutions that ensure access to capital and necessities of life for all
- Designing participatory and accountable governance systems by, for, and of the people

Will those do the trick of turning us into butterflies? *How* will we execute these strategies? When? Where? And most importantly, who will execute them? Which of them are you working on, or to which do you want to dedicate your life?

Action Plans

A New Direction of Time

What a time to be alive! This is it! Everything is up for grabs. The world is challenged by climate chaos, oppression of women, plutocratic political regimes, grossly inadequate health and educational systems, elite capture of fiscal policy, massive unemployment, and tensions among religions and lifestyles.

We are in the midst of a whole systems transformation with no guaranteed outcomes. Will we be a species managed by the superrich and the ideologues or empowered through a self-governing system of learning, creativity, and compassion? Will our societies be focused on surveillance, control, and punishment or on the development of the full potential of every living being? Will we live on a planet of catastrophic suffering? Or will we choose to create a new possibility for life on Earth—a compassionate civilization?

These are the questions. The answers reside in what the seven billion plus of us decide and do in this decade and century. Where do you and I stand? What are we each going to do?

This is the time to manifest our care for life on Earth by being engaged in relieving suffering and catalyzing a new civilization. For me, I am putting my energy into calling forth a future based on six principles—environmental sustainability, gender equality, participatory governance, economic and social justice, cultural tolerance, and nonviolence.

My own efforts include teaching, training, facilitating, consulting, speaking, and writing. I am working to promote innovative leadership for sustainable human development around the world.

My partners are international organizations and the urban and rural poor. What about you? What do you want to be doing?

Work of every sort is needed in all fields and at all levels. We need effective projects, programs, and policies in every sector. We need transformative work within families, communities, municipalities, states, nations, and bioregions and at the planetary level.

We need a movement of movements bringing together all those of goodwill who are driven by a transformative wind. "Not I, not I, but the wind that blows through me! A fine wind is blowing the new direction of time. If only I let it bear me, carry me, if only it carry me!" (D. H. Lawrence, 1994, page 194).

In the midst of our work, we need to have compassion for those trapped in fear and anger over threats to their identity, worldview, and moral sense and for those stuck in greed and pride for the increase of their wealth and power. Compassion, yes, but not capitulation. What is at stake is the very future of the human experiment—of consciousness of consciousness of consciousness.

STOP!

We humans know the difference between right and wrong. It is time to stop doing what is wrong and start doing what is right. Sound simple? It is, and this is what we need to stop, now:

1. Stop extracting, processing, selling, and burning fossil fuels that damage our planetary ecosystem and cause harm to billions of people and other forms of life.

2. Stop all activities that damage Earth's water, air, soil, plants, and animals.

3. Stop passing laws that take away a woman's sovereignty over her own body.

4. Stop paying a woman less than a man for the same work.

5. Stop paying workers a wage that they and their families cannot live on.

6. Stop allowing our fellow human beings to live in poverty.

7. Stop the fiscal, monetary, and economic systems that allow 1 percent of the population to own 43 percent of all assets, and for the bottom 80 percent to own only 6 percent.

8. Stop financial institutions from creating and marketing toxic investments.

9. Stop allowing our children to grow up without an education.

10. Stop denying health care to every person.

11. Stop the filibuster from being used to block virtually every piece of legislation.

12. Stop gerrymandering voting districts that ensure a permanent majority for one party.

13. Stop passing laws that make it difficult or impossible for women, youth, the elderly, and the poor to vote.

14. Stop the government from spying on its citizens.

15. Stop people of one religious belief system from harming people of another tradition.

16. Stop people of one sexual persuasion from harming people of another orientation.

17. Stop people of one race from harming someone of another race.

18. Stop maintaining a prison system that must generate inmates in order to make a profit.
19. Stop allowing the manufacture and selling of arms.
20. Stop attacking and killing people around the world with drones or other means without due process, a UN resolution, or a declaration of war. (In fact, stop harming anyone for any reason by any means.)

We can do what is right by changing our individual minds and behaviors and by transforming our collective cultures and systems. We need a moral awakening that expresses itself in new values, citizen action, policies, and institutions. We can do this, now. But first, we must **STOP**.

———

Ten Pledges of Transformation

I have often felt the need to acknowledge the harm done by my ancestors, my country, and my generation. I confess the following ten wrongdoings, express my regret, and pledge to right these wrongs. These are representative of many, many other such acts:

1. My European ancestors (Scottish) committed genocide of the native peoples of America. I express my deep sorrow and regret. I pledge to support the sovereignty of and make retribution to Native Americans and indigenous peoples around the world.

2. My ancestors participated in the enslavement of Africans brought to America. I (whose Kentucky ancestors had slaves) express my deep sorrow and regret. I pledge to support the equality and empowerment of African Americans and to stop all slavery in any form around the world.

3. My country did not give the right to vote to women during its first 144 years. I express my deep sorrow and regret. I pledge to support the full equality and leadership of women in America and around the world.

4. My country participated in killing hundreds of thousands of people in Vietnam. I express my deep sorrow and regret. I pledge to support peaceful coexistence and nonviolence around the world.

5. My country invaded Iraq without UN permission or just cause, killing hundreds of thousands of people and wasting billions of dollars. I express my deep sorrow and regret. I pledge to support peaceful coexistence and nonviolence around the world.

6. My country sends drones into Afghanistan, Pakistan, and elsewhere, killing thousands of people. I express my deep sorrow and regret. I pledge to support peaceful coexistence and nonviolence around the world.

7. My country does not mandate a living wage for its citizens. I express my deep sorrow and regret. I pledge to promote sustainable livelihoods for all people at home and around the world.

8. My generation has not heeded the call to stop global warming, which has damaged Earth's ecosystems and will cause

harm to billions of people and other living beings. I express my deep sorrow and regret. I pledge to stop the fossil fuel industry and promote climate chaos mitigation and adaptation at home and around the world.

9. My country allows toxic investments to be sold at home and around the world. I express my deep sorrow and regret. I pledge to promote the creation of a new global economy devoted to human dignity and environmental sustainability.

10. My country encourages huge income inequality with the majority of our citizens living in poverty. I express my deep sorrow and regret. I pledge to do everything in my power to create a world of equality, justice, happiness, and well-being for all people and all living beings on planet Earth.

May it be so. So be it.

• • •

In the next chapter, we will identify and reflect upon many more actions to catalyze a compassionate civilization.

CHAPTER 3

THE SIX ARENAS OF TRANSFORMATION

Environmental Sustainability, Gender Equality, Socioeconomic Justice, Participatory Governance, Cultural Tolerance, and Peace and Nonviolence

In this chapter, we will explore the six arenas of transformation and continue to identify needed action, understanding, and motivation that will help us realize a compassionate civilization. Most of these were written between 2013 and 2015.

Environmental Sustainability

Who Will Take Us to Safe Harbor?

The autumn air is crisp and cool, and the blue sky is filled with clear light. Red, yellow, and gold mingle and gleam amid shades of brown. More of the river reappears each day. Last night before the frost, I carried the balcony plants into the living room, where they will live for a while. Winter is coming. Leaves fall to the ground, and trees and landscapes are laid bare. Here in the Hudson Valley, we humans are preparing for snow and ice.

And so it goes year after year, season after season. We know that everything is born, lives, grows old, and dies. And out of the old and bygone, new life bubbles up and erupts with buds and babies. This is the way of life on Earth and, in fact, throughout this vast universe. And yet these days, a new awareness is among us.

With fossil fuel–induced global warming, Earth has changed, and life on Earth is in grave danger. This is not happening because Earth is angry or because we humans are bad. It is happening because what had been a brilliant solution to energy production is having unintended consequences, and the laws of physics and ecosystems are at work. We must once again adjust to a new terrain as we have over the eons. It is too late to stop climate chaos, but we must slow it down and adapt to a new Earth.

This will put massive stresses on our political, economic, and social systems. With the human population already over seven billion and heading toward ten billion, the demands for water, food, shelter, air, jobs, schools, and health care will be huge and will create chaotic scenarios.

Again, this is not happening because we have been bad but because we succeeded in extending human life and creating productive societies around the world. What was, however, can no longer be. A whole systems transformation is underway. As the current unsustainable and unjust civilization crumbles under these pressures, a new civilization will emerge. Will it be a more or a less human and sustainable one? It is up to us, to you and me.

Our every decision and action becomes crucial. How we live, work, shop, vote, speak, lobby, petition, write, and act all become paramount. Are we going to angle toward utopia or settle for dystopia? Will we use this time of crisis and transformation to reinvent human society and create a world that works for everyone, or will we withdraw into our small groups and ourselves? Will the rich try to create their own secure world with the masses of humanity suffering and dying all around them?

It is time for the boldest of visions and the bravest of actions. It is time for someone—anyone, everyone—to right the ship of life and to head for safe harbor for all.

Love at First Sight: Vows to Earth

How did you feel the first time you saw the NASA photograph of Earth? For me and many others, it was love at first sight. In 1969, I traveled around the world for the first time, just three years after that photo was taken, and I fell hopelessly in love with her.

"Earthling Vows"

Earth, our only home
Precious beyond priceless
Gift of the universe
Our mother who gives us life

Earth, our only home
We cherish you and vow
To keep you safe from harm
We swoon at the stunning beauty
Of your land

Earth, our only home
We give you thanks for air and water
We delight in your plants and animals
We celebrate each of your humans

Earth, our only home
We vow to let go of violence and greed
And create a new civilization of
Compassion and understanding
Earth, our only home

Consciousness and Climate Chaos

Human consciousness is reflexive. This is to say, it is aware of itself. But it is not only aware of itself but also aware that it is aware of itself. The question then becomes, does this regression (or progression) go on infinitely? And what does this have to do with compassion and catalyzing a new civilization?

By being aware of our awareness of our awareness, we are in a continuous process of observing sensory data of the world, reflecting on our observations, interpreting our reflections, deciding based on our interpretations, and acting in relation to our decisions. OK, but what does this have to do with climate chaos and the human response?

Some humans (scientists) observe data about the climate and note that temperatures are rising on our planet, causing ice to melt, seas to rise, and coastlines and islands to be submerged. Through reflection on this progression of cause and effect, they feel alarmed at the devastating scenario projected. Their interpretation is that the burning of fossil fuels is causing this dangerous sequence of events. Their decision is to call for an immediate shift from energy derived from fossil fuels to renewable sources that do not produce carbon dioxide and other greenhouse gases.

However, there are other human beings (in corporations) who become alarmed by this conclusion, which if acted upon would mean the loss of trillions of dollars of their assets. This reflection then leads them to interpret climate change as incorrect or an unproven theory or simply highly inconvenient, which leads to their decision and action to fight climate science with false information and outright denial.

However, as other human beings (more and more people) observe the devastation of megastorms, flooding, droughts, mass movements of people, and social chaos, they will become alarmed and ask the question of why this is happening. The answers of empirical cause and effect provided by climate scientists will make more and more sense to more and more people. As this happens, common sense and policy will shift toward immediate large-scale action to stop the use of fossil fuels and make massive investments in renewable energy to abate climate chaos.

With more than fourteen billion eyes, seven billion brains, and fourteen billion hands at work, humanity will move as one to safeguard present and future generations of life on Earth. This process of mass awakening and action, however, needs to speed up before we further damage our planetary ecosystems, causing great harm to vast numbers of living beings. On the count of three, let's wake up and act together. One…two…three.

Are There Too Many People?

After emerging as a species just two hundred thousand years ago (on a planet more than four billion years old), it took 190,000 years to reach one million of us. It then took another 9,700 years (to around the year 1800) to reach one billion of us. Then, in a little over two hundred years, we have reached over seven billion of us today. Projections are that in only thirty-seven more years, there will be at least nine billion people living on Earth (data from UNDESA's Population Division).

What is the carrying capacity of Earth? What is sustainable growth and development? What are the implications for population and ecosystem function?

The consequences of this astronomical human growth are devastating. The ten warmest years on record have occurred since 1998. We face massive shortages of food, water, energy, housing, jobs, and so on. We face tipping points of climate and ecosystem disasters. We cannot technologize our way out of this. We must consume less and conserve more, especially in the industrialized countries.

Scientist and author Stephen Emmott concludes his book *Ten Billion* with these words: "I think we're fu-ked." I am not ready to say that. I am still hopeful. The question is, how in the world are we going to change our mind-sets, behaviors, cultures, and systems in time to avoid even greater disasters and achieve a compassionate civilization?

When the United States entered World War II, President Roosevelt ordered all industries to shift to a war footing and produce armaments. Faced with an external threat after the bombing of Pearl Harbor, the United States mobilized its population and economic machine to do what was necessary to defend freedom.

What would be the parallel today of dramatic collective action? For example, how could the UN call the nations of the world to a sustainable development footing lest we lose not only our freedom but life itself? How can each nation call its people together to do what is necessary? How can each industry and nongovernmental organization (NGO) do what is necessary? How can each individual, you and me, do what is necessary to save life on Earth?

And to the degree that we cannot do this, we should face our fate and begin to grieve our loss.

Every Day Is Earth Day

Every day is Earth day
and always has been,
the only place we
have ever known a day

or night or anything
else at all.
These years, four billion,
two million, two hundred thousand,
five thousand, two thousand,
hooray for our heavenly
home, beautiful beyond
beauty, alive beyond
aliveness, abundant
for all
and yet, and yet
we humans divide and
hoard and pillage and rape
and harm our mother,
our own body;
but now is waking up time
making up time
time to cherish and conserve
for the next one thousand, million,
billion years or so
yes
let's

———

Preparing for Impacts of Climate Chaos

We have work to do to stop pumping carbon into the atmosphere, and we also have to adapt to a climate that has already been altered.

How should you and I plan for the next twenty years, knowing what we do about climate chaos and the consequent environmental, social, economic, and political upheavals?

1. Prepare for reduced food production and increased prices.
2. Prepare for flooding of coastal areas and islands.
3. Prepare for megastorms.
4. Prepare for water shortages.
5. Prepare for droughts and fires.
6. Prepare for the transition from fossil fuels to renewable energy.
7. Prepare for political battles.
8. Prepare for mass migrations.
9. Prepare for economic volatility.

What are implications for one's life choices?

1. Don't live near bodies of water that can rise.
2. Have a small boat.
3. Have access to land to grow or buy fresh food.
4. Have access to fresh water.
5. Have solar panels on the roof of your home.
6. Invest funds in renewable energy, water supply, and food production.
7. Live in an area that is not too hot or too cold.
8. Live in an area with fewer megastorms.
9. Live near family and friends.
10. Live near services and public transportation.
11. Be politically and socially active.

12. Have a spiritual practice.

13. Be engaged in helping others.

14. Be flexible, be grateful, and be happy.

What would you add or change?

We can do this.

———

Climate Chaos, People Power

The UN Climate Summit happened here in New York on September 23. Right before, on September 21, the Climate March arrived in New York and swelled to massive numbers, demanding that world leaders take decisive action now to avert civilizational catastrophe. I was one of those numbers.

I realize again and again that this is my movement. It is about climate chaos mitigation and adaptation, yes—which is enough, given its severity—but it is also about much, much more. It is about creating gender equality, socioeconomic justice, participatory governance, and cultural tolerance. It is about the future of life on Earth. It is about the future of humanity. It is about the future of my grandchildren and their grandchildren. It is about whether we will create a sustainable planetary civilization based on compassion and understanding or a civilization of environmental destruction and human misery.

Go to watchdisruption.com for a movie about this movement, called *Disruption*. I hope you will watch, share with others, and then take personal action. We must manifest our commitment to a viable, ethical future through our voting, our shopping, our values, our speaking, our writing, our activism, our spending, our investments, our reading, our homemaking, our house insulation, our donations, our relationships, our child rearing, our driving, our recycling, our energy sources, our grandparenting, our volunteering, our serving, and our marching.

Here is a link to possibilities of engagement: peoplesclimate.org

Yes, we can. Yes, we must.

The Original People Can Lead Us Home

What is our scientific story of human emergence? Around two hundred thousand years ago, *Homo sapiens* emerged, with *Homo sapiens sapiens* appearing around fifty thousand years ago. We like to say that recorded human history is around five thousand years in duration. What was going on during those previous forty-five thousand or even 195,000 years? What were our ancestors thinking? What were they feeling? What were their struggles, fears, and hopes? What did they love?

As human migrations took place from eastern Africa to other parts of our planet, people began to settle into ecological niches. We adapted to dry deserts, lush vegetation, little islands, and mountain ranges. We became the people of that place, whom we now call aboriginal people, the original people. As empires rose out of Mongolia, Greece, India, and elsewhere, their armies swept over the lands of the original people, conquering and inculcating them into the empire.

Fast-forward to the modern European global conquest. For a number of reasons, the Europeans felt that the world was theirs to be had. They sent out explorers, followed by armies and merchants, conquering the original people of Earth. The Europeans brought their religions and cultures and ways of life, annihilating and subjugating the original people in the name of Crown, Church, and Commerce. They established ownership of the land, enslaved or murdered the original people, and shipped precious minerals and other natural resources back to the fatherland, making Europe very, very wealthy.

And so it went with other nations taking their turns to invade, rape, and impoverish the original people of Earth, spreading toxic industrialization around the planet. Who can save us? How were the original people often able to live in harmony with their environment? What was their understanding that sustained their existence in every clime and ecological zone on this planet for tens of thousands of years? How has the "modern" worldview been able to degrade and destroy the living environment in just three hundred years? Amazing!

The original people know that they are one with the land. They do not and cannot own it. They are part of nature. They cannot conquer it. They are part of the great fabric of life with their sisters and brothers—plants, animals, water, air, minerals, and soil. They know that it is the responsibility of the people to be stewards of the commons, not its conquerors.

Today, we celebrate the original people who thankfully are still present. Even though they have been abused for hundreds of years, they have survived, and their wisdom is still intact. Their presence and voices now awaken everyone to our present moment of crisis and our possibility to be stewards of Earth. Deep thanks to all original people around this planet. Please lead us back home.

———

Gender Equality

Women of the World, Unite!

Men had their chance and blew it—thousands of years of patriarchy, and look at the sad state of the world. Poisoned air and water, ravaged land, resource depletion, colossal waste, acidic oceans, megastorms, flooding, droughts, wildfires, genetically damaged plant life, massive dieback of species, plutocratic governance, economic and social injustice, cultural and religious intolerance—these are the results of unbridled patriarchy. Enough! Women of the world, unite! Throw off your chains, and lead humanity to a compassionate civilization.

For millennia, men and women have been taught that men are the stronger sex and must protect and lead the family and the larger society. This dominator model has become as assumed as the air we breathe. It is in our cultural DNA, but it is a disease. It has left out the wisdom, creativity, and leadership of half of humanity—womankind.

Now that we face multiple crises in every sector of society and are at the end of the current civilization, it is time for a new way of decision-making and governing to be forged and exercised. A genuine partnership of women and men at every level is called for as never before.

In recent years, women have gained the right to vote (can you believe that there was ever a time when this was thought not to be necessary?), with a few examples of women leadership in government and the corporate sector, but far too few. All too often, women hit a glass ceiling with top positions being held by men. This must change.

Studies show that the higher the percentage of women in decision-making positions, the more creative and effective are the outcomes. It is time for men to listen more than speak and to honor the intelligence, insights, and leadership of female counterparts.

Women often place more emphasis on collaboration, cooperation, nurture, relationship, empathy, compassion, care, and intuition than men. This is sorely needed to balance the testosterone-infused aggression, competition, and proud egos of men. Male energy will continue to be needed but must be balanced with female energy, or things will continue to spin out of control.

Men often promote warfare, hyperobjectification, instrumentalism, and agency. These tendencies must be held in check by feminine values and styles of thinking, doing, and being.

What is at stake is the very notion of a social contract and a viable lifestyle on planet Earth. The dominator model must step aside for a collaborative and compassionate way of being. Greed must give way to generosity. Fear and hatred must be overcome by mutual trust and care. Violence must be replaced by peaceful coexistence and cooperation.

My sisters, I am ready to listen, dialogue, collaborate, and follow.

———

The Necessity of Female Leadership

Why are 3.5 billion people discriminated against, controlled, and abused because they are female?

The pervasive power of the patriarchy cannot be overestimated. This is true for both men and women. We have all been sold this same message, and it is wrong.

We can go through the histories of the world's religions that all put forward a story of a male god, a male teacher, a male savior, a male prophet, and a male priesthood. We can point to biological factors—such as the superior physical strength of most men; the sexual roles of penetration and receptivity; and the maternal roles of gestation, giving birth, breastfeeding, and nurturing—requiring men to be protectors and breadwinners. These and other factors are pointed to as proofs or reasons to believe in male dominance. But they are wrong.

We are all human beings first, period. And then we are female or male. All human beings have consciousness, perception, perspective, intelligence, wisdom, capacity, and skill. All human beings need community, food, water, shelter, meaning, education, development, health, engagement, respect, and love. Each and every human being has a unique contribution to make to the civilizing process based on her or his innate potentials and capacities and the development and realization of those potentials.

Because of the past several thousand years of male dominance, however, the gifts, knowledge, wisdom, and style of female human beings have not been allowed to play their full and necessary roles and leadership at all levels of society. Human society has become highly distorted toward male values of aggression, competition, abstraction, control, and detachment. Cutthroat capitalism, obsession with technology, warfare, a culture of violence, and the destruction of the natural world are all features of this tragic distortion.

Without the full expression, partnership, and leadership of feminine knowledge and wisdom, humanity will not make it through this time of crisis to a compassionate civilization but will collapse in endless inequality, human misery, injustice, intolerance, and environmental degradation.

Feminine wisdom can and should be found in men as well. But it is in the voices and actions of women themselves that we must look for new leadership and new hope.

A Tribute to Mothers

Giving birth to new life
Nurturing, sustaining, guiding
Releasing, launching, affirming
Love begetting love
A flow onward
Mother Earth
Mother Tree
Mother Tiger
Mother Eve
My grandmothers,
Sally and Arrie,
My mother, Mary Elizabeth
My children's mother,
Mary
My grandchildren's mother, Jennifer
My grandchildren's grandmother, Bonnie
Baby girls who become young women
Who become leaders of our race

Prime ministers, presidents, priests
CEOs, managers, engineers,
Artists, doctors, astronauts,
Thank you, thank you, thank you
Love upon love
Gratitude upon gratitude
May we each attain Motherhood
Hail!

A Song of Praise

My Aunt Hiahwahnah, member of the Choctaw Nation, lady of dignity and poise, proud, beautiful, intelligent, educated, loving wife and mother, teacher. My Aunt Hiahwahnah. Beloved wife of my father's brother, dear friend of my mother.

I remember when I learned that there were four *h*'s in your name. The caring mother of my four first cousins, Johnny, Pam (PK), Susan, and Merrilee. We used to play together in Grandmother Work's front yard in Henryetta, Oklahoma, dressed up as cowboys and Indians. We would also drive up the steep hill to your house and play.

Ninety-five years—that's a long time to live, laugh, love, see, think, and feel. How can you be gone? We miss you too much. Yet you are still here in our hearts, cells, and memories. I feel your strength, determination, clarity, and passion.

Your children, grandchildren, and great-grandchildren have so much love for you in their hearts. You are legend. You are ancestor.

You are great mother. And as your nephew, I sing a song of praise and honor for your life and spirit.

Thank you, dearest Aunt. Thank you for a long life well lived. I am grateful that I was with you eleven months ago in Oklahoma. I am grateful that you passed peacefully. I am grateful for my wonderful tribe of cousins. I love you. Farewell. Happiness and peace be yours forever.

———

Socioeconomic Justice

Money, Money, Money

Money, money, money,
Always sunny,
In the rich man's world.

So go the lyrics of the Abba song. What about for you and me? What is the reality of money? Whether you are part of the 1 percent or the 99 percent makes all the difference in how you view money.

One way the rich make money with money is by placing bets in the global gambling casino called the stock market. Making more money can become an addiction, an obsession. Desire and greed can be insatiable. It seems you can never get enough. You always need more. The poor and the middle class, on the other hand, usually make money with their labor, time, energy, and intelligence. But they would agree with the rich that you never have enough and that you always need more.

But what is money anyway? It began as a means of exchange—a symbol—of goods and services between and among people. However, over time and with the invention of interest, dividends, and debt, it became an end in itself, an abstraction no longer attached to goods, services, people, or nature—a self-referencing value system. Money is now no more than electronic information, numbers on a computer screen.

If you have it, it can multiply. If you don't, there is no guarantee you ever will. It is the stuff you need to play the game of living. Even though you can't eat, drink, or breathe money, without it, you may not be able to eat, drink, or breathe at all. Therefore, if you want to live, you must either receive a wage from someone who has money to pay you or borrow money from someone who has money to loan you and then pay the loan back (principal plus interest).

We now live in a world of staggering inequality where a few people own and control the money supply. With this, they can buy as much of whatever they wish—land, housing, water, food, natural resources, labor, the means of production, the levers of government, media, and so forth—and make some of it available to the masses of humanity through wages and debt, thus maintaining inequality endlessly.

This is not right. It is not just. It is not the human way of compassion. We must fundamentally reinvent fiscal and monetary policy and economic relationships. Money must be reunited with its original ground of valuation—the well-being of all the people and of the natural world of water, land, air, plants, and animals.

We need a new paradigm of money based in abundance, not scarcity; in generosity, not hoarding; in equality and justice; and in promoting gross national happiness. Money must be redesigned in a way that protects the natural environment and ensures the well-being of all people everywhere. This is the human way, the way of compassion.

———

Economic Fairness Is Necessary

This is a tough one. Corporations do rule the world, as author David Korten reminds us. What can we do when faced with the biggest of all the giants, the one that believes it deserves to rule? Corporations control politics, media, natural resources, employment, and fiscal policy. They create desire through advertising that keeps the consumption-production machine running at top speed. We are entrained to consume more and therefore to produce more. This is the definition of progress, GNP, GDP, and it is killing Earth and enslaving humanity.

How do we break the trance? Gross national happiness (GNH) has arrived at the right time. The meaning of life is not found in owning the latest gadget. It is found in caring relationships, awareness, learning, creativity, good health, and contemplation of nature. Sam Cooke's song by the same name is right; "the best things in life are free" (or should be available to everyone).

How then do we redress this tyrannical imbalance of the social order? We must start, as usual, with ourselves, you and me. We can practice voluntary simplicity as a model for others. We can get our priorities straight. We can rebalance our own lives, with care of others as a top priority. We can bring our saving, spending, and borrowing under control.

At the policy level, we must require corporations to pay a living wage with adequate benefits. Workers should enjoy a share of profits. Customers must be protected from products that are harmful. CEOs should not make more than ten to fifty times a regular salary. Currently in the US, the average is 204 times more, and some are as high as 1,800 percent more! Corporations must be held to the highest standards of environmental protection. Corporations should not be allowed to have a monopoly on life essentials, such as water and food, which must be available to all.

We must get corporate dollars out of politics. Democracy is not for sale; it is a sacred trust of, by, and for the people. Investments must be made safe and fair. Fiscal policy must protect people from being taken advantage of by lenders. Monetary policy must place controls on interest and dividends. Appropriate levels of taxation of corporations must be practiced. Some currently pay none.

We must remember what an economy is for. Its bottom line is not money but the well-being of people and nature. Profit is secondary. Astronomical profit for a few is an aberration. Millionaires and billionaires should be taxed at appropriate levels. Under President Eisenhower, it was 91 percent. We are all in this together. There is only one Earth and one human race. The social contract is even more sacred than any constitution. We depend on each other and must care for each other. It is possible to create fairness, and it is a necessary and central feature of a compassionate civilization.

Time to Turn Around

Will someone please explain why an impoverished person goes to jail for stealing ten dollars, but huge corporations that tank the global economy and harm millions of people get a taxpayer bailout? Why does a nation's president who orders the invasion of a sovereign country (based on misinformation fed to the public), wastes billions of taxpayer dollars, and kills tens of thousands of people in the process get to retire to his ranch, publish his memoirs, and conduct speaking engagements?

Why are corporations allowed to make billions of dollars while spewing carbon dioxide into the atmosphere, creating global warming that kills thousands of people from megastorms and will eventually harm billions of people? Why must people have a test and get an official license to drive a car or an official ID to vote but not to buy a military-style automatic weapon on the Internet?

Why do women who work the same jobs as men get paid less? Why doesn't a representational democracy pass laws that are favored by 80 percent of the population? Why are corporations allowed to damage the water table through fracking, the air we breathe through industrial pollution, and the only land we will ever have through strip mining?

Why does *prolife* mean that a fetus has more right to live than the woman bearing it, but if and when it is born, it has no rights to health care, food, or shelter? Why can a white president get away with saying "If you are not for me, you are for the terrorists" while a black president who tries to get health care for forty million low-income Americans is called a Socialist or a Nazi?

Why can a few people live in a $200 million home and millions of human beings live in shacks or on the street? Why do nations spend trillions of dollars on armaments and war but do not have money for educating their children? Why are there billions of dollars to create a new electronic gadget but no funds to eradicate global poverty?

Something is very, very wrong with this picture. The system is utterly corrupt and confused. And we have met the system, and it is us. It is time to have compassion for ourselves, for our own confusion. It is time for the birth of a new way of thinking, doing, and being. May people of goodwill everywhere wake up, turn around, and help catalyze a better world for all people and all life on Earth.

———

Overcoming Four Types of Poverty

There are many types of poverty. Physical, emotional, mental, and spiritual poverty are four of them. Physical poverty can involve hunger and homelessness but also inadequate education, health, economic opportunity, political influence, and environmental safety. Emotional poverty can include an inability to express one's own emotions or to understand or empathize with another's emotions. Mental poverty can involve a deficiency of concepts, language, information, knowledge, analysis, or experience. Spiritual poverty can include an inability to be aware of the good, the true, the beautiful, and the sublime, as well as an inability to transcend one's own ego and to care deeply for others out of compassion and wisdom.

Some people may experience all four types of poverty, whereas others may experience two, three, or only one. A person can be physically poor but rich in emotional, mental, and spiritual prowess. Physical poverty can make it difficult, however, to achieve these other capabilities. If someone is rich materially but is poor emotionally, mentally, and spiritually, he or she will not be able to empathize or care for those trapped in physical poverty.

This is one of the great divides in our societies. People who are rich only in material resources are often not capable of understanding or loving those who suffer from physical poverty. Empirical studies show that with wealth often comes a deficiency of empathy and generosity. Rich people may often be proud and protective of their wealth and may tend not to share it, whereas poor people are often empathic and generous with each other. They know what their own deprivation feels like and can understand others who share this condition and desire to help them.

One question is, how can the materially rich be helped to develop their emotional, mental, and spiritual capacities? But another urgent question is, how can a society directly assist those trapped, some for generations, in impoverished conditions? Since this poverty is a function of a system of inequality and injustice, it must be addressed systemically through new policies, programs, projects, and cultural values that change the rules of the game and provide opportunities and resources directly to the poor. This approach can work to strengthen the entire society by creating a more educated, healthy, productive, and happy population.

———

The Superrich and We the People

What do you do when the whole system is sick, and you are part of it? We live in a world owned and controlled by the superrich. What the superrich want, the superrich get. And what they want is all of it—all the wealth, all the power, all the stuff, all the earth.

They have bought the institutions of democracy—the courts, legislatures, executives, voting, and media. They have bought the water, the land, and the food supply. They control the money supply and monetary and fiscal policy. They own the health care system—the drug companies, the hospitals, and health care policy. They own the educational system—the textbooks, the equipment, and educational policy. They own the places we must work to earn money to survive in the system they have engineered.

They own the companies that pump carbon dioxide into the atmosphere, creating havoc and damaging Earth's ecosystems. They own the companies that make the guns and other weapons that people use to kill each other. They control the government agencies and companies that are spying on citizens and erasing the very notion of privacy. They own the media and entertainment companies that provide the images, "facts," and stories that people live out of.

What else can they own and control? What else do they want? There must always be something more to acquire—more wealth, more power, and more to control. In the past, kings, priests, and generals ruled. Today, CEOs, shareholders, investment bankers, hedge fund managers, and billionaires rule. And what about us, the "little" people? Who are we? What is our lot, our possibility? What can we do about our situation and our lives? Where is our freedom to choose and to create our lives?

In the past, ordinary people overthrew their oppressors with protests and revolutions. What will work today? We must work diligently to awaken minds and hearts, to change individual behavior, to transform cultural values and practices, and to invent new institutions and new policies based on principles of sustainability, equality, justice, participation, and tolerance. We must make use of brilliant strategies and effective tactics. And our means must be the same as our ends. We must use the transforming power of truth and love, compassion and wisdom, peace and happiness.

———

Is Your Life Worth Fifty Cents?

If you are rich (especially "white"), your life is worth a lot, and you are too big to jail. If you are poor (especially "black"), your life is worth little, and you are ready for jail and ripe to be killed.

Eric Garner—forty-three, father, husband, American citizen, child of God—was trying to sell cigarettes for fifty cents each. This is not legal, so several white policemen approached him. They swarmed him and pressed his head into the sidewalk. "I can't breathe," he said repeatedly until he choked to death. The breath of life, breathing in and breathing out, is a focus of meditation and enlightenment. When I saw the video of his murder, I was horror struck and gasped for breath. The grand jury recommended no trial. His life was worth fifty cents.

Michael Brown—eighteen years old, African American, unarmed—was shot to death by a white policeman with twelve bullets. The policeman said that the boy looked like a "demon." The grand jury recommended no trial.

Tamir Rice—twelve years old, African American—was playing alone in a public park with a pellet gun. A white policeman shot and killed him two seconds after encountering him. Will there be justice?

What is a human life worth? What is a human being? Are we spiritual beings having a human experience, as Chardin said? Do we each have a unique gift to be realized and contributed to the civilizing process? Are we each an Einstein or a Mother Teresa in hiding?

And what is justice? Is it only for the rich and powerful? Do we live in a police state? Is our democracy of, by, and for the people dead and gone? Is there any hope for a resurrection?

Systemic racism is alive and well. And race doesn't even exist. We are all part of the human race, one singular species. And then there is sexism, homophobia, classism, religious fundamentalism, nationalism, ethnic prejudice, and ageism.

It all begins with ignorance, which leads to a sense of separateness, which leads to pride, which leads to greed, which leads to fear, which leads to anger, which leads to hatred, which leads to violence. Cut the flow of cause and effect. Cut it now. Awaken to compassion and wisdom!

The Empire: Bow Down or Rise Up?

How do we wake up and change our ways? That is the question. How do we wake up to the fact that we are destroying billions of years of life on Earth and turning a blind eye to the suffering of our fellow and sister human beings because of our ignorance, fear, and greed?

And when we wake up, what should we do? How can we facilitate or lead in acts of repentance, which means turning around and going in a new direction? What will turn the tide? Teaching meditation? Publishing books? Having a TV show? Doing seminars? Teaching grad students? Caring for the homeless? Marching? Voting? Installing solar panels on the roof? Caring for the grandchildren? All of these? Any of this? Something else?

And who are the deluded forces we face? Fossil fuel companies, banks, armaments companies, toxic-food companies, stock markets, billionaires, millionaires, and religious fundamentalists are a few of them.

There is so much suffering in the world. It is overwhelming. How can we go on, moment by moment? Where is hope? Where is joy? The good news is that whatever we do, there will still be suffering, and everyone will still die. That is the way life is, at least in this part of the galaxy. We shouldn't feel like failures for not being able to get rid of all suffering and death. But we can do a lot. How can we best relieve suffering and embrace death by living with open eyes and a joyous heart?

We are waking up to the reality that we live in a global empire controlled by and for the wealthy and their corporations. That is real. That is true. It is our empire. People before us lived in other empires, such as the British Empire, the Ottoman Empire, the Roman Empire, the Mongol Empire, the various dynasties of China, and so on. Ours is the Global Corporate Empire of the 1 percent. Welcome to our times. Welcome home, child of the empire.

We each have a choice: bow our head and be a loyal subject of the empire, or raise our eyes and challenge the empire with our thoughts, words, and deeds. Whichever you choose, don't forget to enjoy your one wild, ecstatic life.

———

Participatory Governance

Dysfunctional Politics to Participatory Governance: Krugman, Wilber, and Me

Paul Krugman of the *New York Times* wrote that "politics determines who has the power, not who has the truth." Many would say that politics is the art of the possible. I believe that politics itself is dysfunctional, is leading us to disaster, and must be completely reinvented. This is as true in the United States as it is anywhere.

The politics of personality and persuasion, of command and control, makes it impossible for the collective intelligence of 7.3 billion people to be applied to our most pressing problems. To paraphrase Ken Wilber, as I did in 1997 in the UN's first policy paper on governance, humanity's greatest challenges are not climate change and poverty but our inability to achieve "mutual understanding and mutual agreement concerning means for dealing quickly and effectively with the profound threats to the well-being of people everywhere and to the environment." This is a crisis of governance. Politics has become a dangerous game blocking us from mutual understanding, agreement, and action.

We must shift to a political process of authenticity and substance based on principles of truth and well-being for all. We must shift to a modus operandi of participatory governance for sustainable human development. Governance includes government but goes beyond it to include civil society and the private sector. It is through the healthy interaction of these three actors that societies can best protect the environment, promote socioeconomic development, ensure gender equality, and achieve cultural and religious tolerance and understanding.

It is by enabling the voices and concerns of every citizen to be heard and felt in policy-making and implementation that we can best achieve sustainable human development. The perceptions and priorities of scientists, women, students, elders, workers, parents, business leaders, academics, journalists, minorities, religious leaders, artists, the homeless, civil servants, and others must all flow into and guide the governing processes.

Of course, there are many obstacles that can block this shift to participatory governance for sustainable human development. Vested interests of all sorts must be dealt with. When we the people identify corruption based on greed or harmful behavior based on fear, anger, and hatred, we must shine a light on the people involved and call them to account for and change their ways. Truth and reconciliation are powerful transformative processes, as we saw in South Africa after the end of apartheid.

There is a pathway. But what other strategies will carry us forward? How do we get from dysfunctional politics to participatory governance?

We must first tell the truth that things are not working and that there is a systems failure. Then, we must outline a future vision as we have begun above. We must ask everyone to participate in fleshing out that vision with his or her best insights. We must ask people to identify the biggest obstacles that we face. We must ask people to create strategies, tactics, and action plans for reinventing our societal decision-making and action-taking.

We can do this. We must do this or continue careening toward the abyss.

Yes!

Public Administration Capacity Building

The following is a summary of my paper for the UN Economic and Social Council, "Strengthening Governance and Public Administration Capacities for Development" (2007).

> From time to time, one sees the possibility of the world as it could be, where each of us has the opportunity to live life fully and to have our lives make the kind of difference we want to make. Focusing our attention, daily and hourly, not on what is wrong but on what we love and value, allows us to participate in the birth of a better future, ushered in by the choices we make each and every day.
>
> —Nelson Mandela

How can public administration and development practitioners better engage in governance and development to relieve human suffering, protect Earth's fragile ecosystems, and reframe societal goals for peace and progress? It is now understood that institutional and human capacities, governance, and development are interdependent and in a relationship of mutual cause and effect.

In this time of radical transformation and crisis, a new generation of governance and public administration capacities is needed to achieve sustainable, people-centered, pro-poor governance and development. This includes abilities to think and act comprehensively and in consideration of future generations, effectively and collaboratively, ethically and with self-awareness, creatively and courageously, and in the collective interest and stewardship of the global commons.

Governance and public administration capacities are needed to design and develop systems, institutions, and policies; facilitate effective organizations, networks, teams, communities, and projects; reinterpret cultural values and stories; re-create national vision and social communication; and enhance individual awareness, values, and practical skills.

Each governance and public administration institution faces capacity challenges in relation to the internationally agreed development goals, including the Millennium Development Goals (and later, the Sustainable Development Goals,) with special challenges present in countries responding to rapid system change and trauma. Assessment of current capacities needs to be carried out in an inclusive and participatory manner and become the basis for capacity development planning and implementation.

Practical tools and modalities of governance and public administration capacities can help accelerate and deepen human and ecologically sound development, especially in situations where there has been conflict or disaster. Some examples of these capacities include systems thinking and management, strategic action planning, social mobilization to create a basis for trust and reconciliation, building coalitions, creation of new stories of hope and development, methods for expanding creativity, and sustained motivation promoting national cohesion and harnessing information and communication technologies (ICTs) and knowledge management for development.

From these considerations, key recommendations can be made to strengthen governance and public administration capacities for UN member states, the UN Economic and Social Council, and the

UN Secretariat. Support for innovative approaches to capacity development is especially important. The success of such approaches can introduce new or improved governance and public administration capacities for development.

———

How to Resuscitate Dead Democracy

American democracy is badly broken and may already be dead. What went wrong? How did it come to this sad state of affairs? Polarization and money are two of the mass murderers.

How can the vast array of views of 317 million people be reduced to only two—Democrat or Republican? This is indeed radical reductionism. The world then becomes bifurcated into black and white, red or blue, with good and bad being applied appropriately. But what are these two views/parties anyway? How do they so amazingly allow the country to be set into two warring camps? Republican views are often based on fear—fear of the other, fear of losing privilege—and are an amalgam of the wealthy and religious fundamentalists. Democratic views are often based on inclusion and a belief that everyone should have a fair chance. But is this the whole story?

The wizard behind the curtain is the oligarchy, the superrich. The political process becomes a charade of attack ads and big data while bankers, fossil fuel magnates, and other billionaires pull the levers. To get elected, candidates must have money to buy advertising. The money comes from the wealthy and goes to advertising firms owned by the wealthy—a win-win proposition. The wealthy then own the politicians. The wealthy then send their lobbyist to Washington to write the laws. And so we have a happy ending. The two opposing camps are really serving one master. All is well. Corporate bailouts will continue. Social programs will be cut. Infrastructure will collapse. Global warming will accelerate. Perpetual war will be waged. The global elite will remain happy and in control because capital is global and can always find places to make a profit. So, the two parties are really two faces of the one party of the superrich. Is there any hope?

Yes, we the people must speak, write, organize, vote, purchase, donate, invest, and act in a million ways each day. The key to a healthy democracy is citizen participation. How you and I participate in society is crucial. We can repair the social contract with our every word and deed. We can manifest our care for those in need. We can help give voice to the voiceless. We can acknowledge our current state of affairs and foster dialogue and action among people from the grassroots to the national and global levels.

We must call the superrich to give up greed for generosity. We must invite religious fundamentalists to return to their traditions' teachings of compassion and care for the vulnerable. We must show the gun lobby that arming a society promotes ever-more danger and death. We must awaken the fossil fuel industry to pivot to green energy. We must entreat the military-industrial complex to use its vast power to create peace and development.

Vote as if your life depends on it, because it does. But don't stop at voting. We must heal the body politic in a million ways. The future of life on Earth is at stake, and we each can make a critical difference.

E-government Promotes Citizen Participation

The following is a brief excerpt of a speech given in Bahrain at a UN global forum on public service in 2013.

E-government can make access to services closer to citizens and bring citizen choices and wisdom into the policy-making process. E-government is one aspect of participatory governance and as such has an important role to play in promoting environmental sustainability, gender equality, and socioeconomic justice. E-government should make citizens aware of the crisis we face in our ecosystems of air, water, soil, plants, and animals and what needs to be done by all citizens to protect the environment and ensure a sustainable ecosystem for millions of years to come. E-government must deal with both mitigation and adaptation to climate chaos. E-government should also promote gender equality by giving voice to women in policy-making and leadership at every level of society. E-government should promote socioeconomic justice by making services of education, health, skills training, credit, and marketing accessible to all citizens.

To close the digital divide, governments should ensure that every citizen has access to computers, smartphones, literacy, and electricity to participate in e-governance. Governments must also ensure that the views of citizens through e-government channels are taken with the greatest of seriousness in policy-making and service delivery. Governments must be held accountable for corruption and must act in a transparent manner. Anything less than this would make e-government and e-governance technical glitter and a sham.

———

Meltdown, Shutdown, What's Next? Or, the Marriage of the Superrich and Religious Fundamentalists

Economic meltdown in 2008, government shutdown in 2013—what will be destroyed next? What is behind these two crises? How are they related to climate chaos; racial, sexual, cultural, and religious intolerance; and social indifference? Our fragile species is having a time of it on our little planet, yes?

The economic meltdown was the result of the greed of wealthy individuals and the financial sector, primarily investment firms, banks, and insurance companies. They invented toxic instruments that were not backed by real assets or real production. When those collapsed, the federal government was used to apply citizen (taxpayer) debt to bail them out, or else.

Next, we found ourselves in a government shutdown that was the result of social, economic, and environmental indifference and hostility to the sick, the elderly, the young, the poor, and even the middle class. It is born from the marriage of an unlikely couple: the superrich and religious fundamentalists.

The superrich, including most prominently the fossil fuel industry, despise the federal government for any attempt to respond to climate chaos that would endanger their asset base and their profits. But it also includes all the superrich who do not want to be taxed to pay for health, education, and infrastructure for the masses.

Religious fundamentalists, on the other hand, hate the federal government for its support of the equality and rights of the different races (e.g., blacks and Hispanics), sexes (i.e., women), and different sexual orientations (e.g., homosexual marriage).

Their shared fear and hatred of how the federal government has and could hurt their trust funds or their prejudice and moralism is what has brought about the unholy political marriage of the super-rich and religious fundamentalists. For them, the primary roles of the federal government are two: (1) to have massive military capability to protect the interests of US corporations around the world and (2) to have policies, a police force, and a penal system at home to control and subjugate women, youth, the elderly, the poor, homosexuals, blacks, Hispanics, climate activists, and liberals.

I truly wish all the above were just paranoid delusion rather than naked truth. But there is hope where there is truth and a vision of a better world for all the people and the entire planet.

May we each speak, write, organize, act, and stand our ground with compassion for those who suffer from greed, fear, and hatred but most especially for the least, the lost, and the last.

New Ethic of Public and Private

There is much confusion regarding the distinction between what is public and what is private. In fact, what is public has become distorted into being private, and what is private has become distorted into being public.

New revelations occur frequently concerning how both public sector agencies and private corporations spy on citizens and collect their private data from the Internet and phones for use in antiterrorism and advertising. On the other hand, private corporations own huge industrial farms, produce most of the public's food, and are buying up freshwater sources with the intent of creating a monopoly.

We must recover both public and private realms. The public sphere or the commons has to do with what should rightfully be controlled by and accessible to all citizens. These public goods are necessary for the life and well-being of all citizens, such as land, water, air, food, housing, health, and education. The private sphere has to do with what should rightfully be controlled by and accessible to individual citizens, such as their personal communications, living space, personal information, and choices of belief and lifestyle.

Before the concept of private ownership was enshrined in law, all persons had access to land, water, air, plants, and animals. These gifts of nature were freely available and accessible. When human beings began dividing land and declaring that individuals owned portions, confusion and conflicts began. The invention of money worked in tandem with the invention of private ownership of land. With wealth, things could be bought. And with unlimited wealth, unlimited things could be bought, thus locking away more public goods in private hands.

For example, when Europeans invaded, say, a part of Africa, they would declare the land to be theirs. They would then turn to native Africans and ask, "Would you like to buy some land? If so, you must work in our mines digging up the diamonds that also belong to us and which we will sell." In one gesture, Europeans had stolen African public goods of land and minerals to generate monetary wealth for Europeans that could in turn buy more land or anything else they wished. And so it went, and so it goes. And it is wrong.

If someone comes to your home and tells you that he is now the owner, you would tell him that he is crazy, and you would call the police. However, in the case of public goods around the world, there were no police, and the crazy persons were armed and dangerous and would kill anyone who got in their way. This is the way of the conqueror and the colonizer. It is a form of armed robbery in the name of whomever or whatever—the Crown, God, or Capital.

This wrongdoing has gone on so long that it is now assumed to be reasonable and right. It is neither. It is immoral and based on greed and a complete negation of empathy. We must do better. We must change our ways of thinking and behaving. We must recover the commons and protect the rights of each individual and of nature. Later on, we will explore how this might be done.

Vote Today for Twenty Opportunities for All

On Election Day, what time will you go to the polls? How will you get there? What could interrupt your voting? How would you still vote? Whom can you take with you? Whom can you urge to vote?

It is crucial to vote for opportunity for all, not opposition to all. Twenty opportunities for all include the following:

1. A woman's right to the sanctity and autonomy of her body
2. A woman's right for equal pay for equal work
3. A citizen's right to vote
4. A citizen's right to participate in policy-making
5. A citizen's right to his or her religious beliefs and practices

6. A worker's right to a living wage
7. A person's right to marry the person he or she loves
8. A community's right to safety and security through gun regulations
9. An elder's right to Social Security and Medicare
10. A low-income person's right to Medicaid
11. A student's right to a low-interest student loan
12. A young black man's right to be in public with safety and respect
13. A nation's right to peace, not perpetual war
14. A nation's right to progressive taxation
15. A nation's right to a sustainable environment and climate
16. A nation's right to safe food and medicine
17. A nation's right to health care and quality education for all
18. A nation's right to a strong social contract
19. A nation's right to sustainable infrastructure
20. A nation's right to decentralized, green energy

We humans have been voting since the sixth century BC in Athens. Let's keep it up!

Happy voting!

––––––––

Political Grieving, Self-Care, Learning, and Gratitude

When we experience loss, whether it is the death of a loved one or the loss of an election, grieving includes disbelief and anger in addition to sadness and a sense of abandonment. To move on, we must let grief take its natural course. Then, we must let go and get on with living in a new reality.

We must also take care of our wounded heart. We should get sufficient rest and nourishment, take time for ourselves in reading and reflection, and stay in touch with family and friends. Furthermore, we should engage in soul-searching and analysis so that we learn as much as possible from the situation for the sake of future engagements. We then should apply our lessons by modifying our behavior and actions in future situations and relationships.

Finally, we should take comfort by experiencing deep gratitude for the gift of life itself and for our unique life as it unfolds in mystery and perfection.

In the case of recent US elections, some of us, me included, are grieving. I can't believe that the rout was so bad. I am angry that certain personalities now have even more power. I am sad that millions of people could be harmed by new policies, especially women, the elderly, students, the poor, the middle class, gays, and immigrants. I feel a strange sense of forlornness. What are your emotions?

How am I to take care of my wounded heart in this situation? I will make sure that I get enough rest and eat healthy food. I will do some reading related to my work and spiritual life. I will have conversations with my spouse about what is going on. She has already sent me an article from the *New Yorker* that cheered me up. How will you care for yourself?

In terms of soul-searching and analysis, I am reading about the election and what we may face over the next two years. I am deciding how I will be more engaged as a citizen from the local to national levels. I will write blog posts and articles, contact my representatives regarding issues, sign petitions, donate to candidates and nongovernmental organizations (NGOs), speak with my students and colleagues, and engage in dialogue with people of other points of view. I will focus especially on supporting climate chaos mitigation and women's empowerment but also on promoting socioeconomic justice, cultural and religious tolerance, and participatory governance. How will you go about your soul-searching?

Finally, I am comforted by deep gratitude for life itself: for my life; for family, friends, and colleagues; for opportunities for engagement and service; for health; and for my spiritual practice. Please consider making a list of what you are grateful for.

May everyone everywhere realize the great happiness that embraces both the ups and the downs of living by saying yes!

———

Let Democratic Dialogue Go Viral

What if governance were an ongoing conversation involving every citizen? What if governance were direct and participatory rather than representational and elitist? What if ensuring inclusion of the intelligence, wisdom, knowledge, perspectives, and perceptions of every citizen made governance processes and outcomes more just, effective, innovative, and sustainable?

This is possible and has become necessary. Without the full participation of the entire human family in policy-making and program implementation, our human systems of governance and development will continue to be flawed, elitist, corrupt, unjust, impoverished, and harmful to life on Earth.

We can and must do this. We can catalyze democratic dialogue at every level—local, city, county, state, nation, region, and planet. Trusted conversations can and must happen anywhere, anytime, with anyone and everyone. Trusted Sharing (www.trustedsharing.com), a revolutionary new app, has arrived to help make this a reality.

I am in conversation with the UN's e-governance branch about this. But you don't have to wait. Right now, you can begin to share your views with other citizens and with the government. Click on the above link and start your own conversation (it's free) about an issue that concerns you. Invite your family, friends, neighbors, and colleagues, and invite people in government, nonprofits, and the private sector. Then, as American scholar Willis Harman famously said, "Don't just do something, get out there and talk." (And don't forget to listen.)

Or, if you would rather, join a conversation about large-scale online conversations that is happening on Trusted Sharing.

Let *democratic dialogue* spread throughout the land and around our home planet!

My Endorsement of Senator Bernie Sanders

This was written before the Democratic Party primary in 2016.

I am supporting and voting for Senator Bernie Sanders in the North Carolina Democratic primary next month. Bernie is a person of life-long integrity and unflagging commitment to social justice. He is the only presidential candidate whose campaign is funded entirely by small donations from ordinary Americans rather than from corporations and wealthy individuals.

I agree with him that we need to break up the big banks, pay for universal Medicare and college education for all with our tax revenue, reform the prison and policing systems, decriminalize marijuana, throw out Citizens United and reform campaign financing, prioritize rapid and massive renewable energy and mitigate climate change, and elect a Progressive Senate and House through massive voter turnout and a political revolution.

I agree with Bernie that we need to strengthen Social Security through taxation on higher incomes; make war our very last choice; foster dialogue with our enemies; pass immigration reform with a pathway to citizenship; pay women the same as men; raise the minimum wage to a living wage of fifteen dollars per hour; establish paid family leave; launch a massive infrastructure building program creating millions of jobs; strengthen veterans care; and promote a culture of tolerance of different races, religions, and sexual orientations.

Bernie has thirty-two years of experience serving the public as mayor, congressman, and senator. Bernie is known as the Amendment King in Congress because he has sponsored the largest number of amendments and knows how to get things done. I believe in Bernie and trust him to inspire us with his compassion and to mobilize the American people to achieve greater equality, justice, sustainability, participation, tolerance, and peace. And the polls show that he is electable and can beat his Republican rival in November. However, if Hillary Clinton turns out to be our candidate, I will fight for her with everything I've got.

———

Cultural Tolerance

Tolerance, Tribalism, and Truth

What are your assumptions? Do you assume that every human who shows up on planet Earth deserves to live, or do you believe that only certain people or certain types of people deserve life? This is a very important distinction from which flows either (1) tolerance, understanding, love, and mutual support or (2) intolerance, judgment, hatred, and death.

According to Google definitions, tolerance is "the ability or willingness to accept something, in particular the existence of opinions or behavior with which one does not necessarily agree." Tolerance is an essential characteristic of pluralistic democracy and a necessity for peaceful coexistence of different peoples. Otherwise, we have varying forms of tribalism that espouse that anyone not of a particular tribe is not human and does not deserve to live. Tolerance doesn't require understanding, approval, or love, only acceptance of another's right to exist. Can't we offer that to each other?

If you say that the only people who should live are Christians, whites, the wealthy, Americans, or heterosexuals, you subscribe to tribalism. Tribalism was perhaps needed thousands of years ago. But in this planetary, interconnected age, it does not work and is a grave danger to world peace, sustainability, and justice.

The profound questions that get raised, and that we touched on in the prologue to this book, are, what is a human being, and why on Earth are we here? Are we intelligent animals, consumers and producers, citizens of the state, children of God, compassionate and wise beings, a star's way of looking at a star, consciousness of consciousness of consciousness—or are we something else? Take utmost care. From your truthful answer, flow your actions toward all people everywhere and, in fact, determine what kind of human being you are.

————

Privilege, Power, Pride, and Prejudice

Pride and Prejudice is a novel written by Jane Austen published in 1813. It deals with conflict and love between the classes in the nineteenth century. It also names what is going on throughout human history, including our own times. We see on every front that those with privilege and power are proud, and that pride often leads to prejudice against those without privilege and power.

Many men are prideful and prejudiced against, dominant over, and harmful toward women. The favored race is often proud and prejudiced against, dominant over, and harmful toward other races. The rich can tend to be prideful and prejudiced against, dominant over, and harmful toward the poor. Ethnic elites are usually proud and prejudiced against, dominant over, and harmful toward other ethnic groups. Religious elites are most often prideful and prejudiced against, dominant over, and harmful toward other religions. Straight people can be proud and prejudiced against, dominant over, and harmful toward gay people.

Our names for the above are misogyny, racism, classism, ethnic demonizing, religious fundamentalism, and homophobia. But the common denominator in all of them is that those with privilege and power risk dominating or doing harm to those with less privilege and power.

What can we do to wake up from this nightmare and create societies of universal equality, justice, participation, tolerance, and sustainability? We must change our mind-sets, behaviors, cultures, and systems from exclusion to inclusion, from pride to compassion, from prejudice to respect, from domination to collaboration, and from doing harm to doing acts of kindness.

How do we do that? First, we must each practice new ways of thinking, doing, and being, moment by moment, for the rest of our lives. Then, we must reinvent the human enterprise itself, based on values of universal compassion and wisdom. Next, we must change our political, economic, social, cultural, and environmental systems. Finally, we must create and offer new education, spiritual teaching, and meditation; new leadership, motivation, and incentives; new symbols, rituals, and stories; and new policies, institutions, and projects.

May it be so.

What Is a Woman? Who Can Be Black?

First and foremost, we are each a human being. Then, we are a sex, a gender, a sexual orientation, an age, a cultural expression, a race, an ethnicity, a linguistic participant, part of an economic class, a nationality, a religious affiliation, a personality type, an educational level, a health condition, a political persuasion, and so on. Beyond and deeper than these broad and sometimes superficial categories of identity, we each fashion a complex and unique self-narrative and image that is ours alone.

Our news commentators and some of the public are excited these days about questions of who is a woman and who is black, and what is a woman and what it means to be black. But they are missing a fundamental point. We are all human beings who suffer and desire happiness and relief from our suffering. Yet in our societies, we use identity to include or exclude and to promote or punish. Identity is a social construct, a mass perception, and a device of power and control.

The irony is that at the deepest level, there is no separate, static self at all but only ontological interdependence, impermanence, and mutual causality. I am because you are. You are because I am. We are all the same, and yet we are each different. We each change continuously. We encounter this mystery of life and death together. We each suffer, and we can help relieve each other's suffering. Kindness and understanding are all that is called for.

Can we not find our way simply to know, do, and be these two responses to each and every living being? For isn't the only lasting "identity" found in values embodied and actions taken?

Let Wedding Bells Ring!

What if we won't give up on love? What if love were the answer? It sounds so simple, maybe even stupid. What if it were true? What does it mean anyway?

Not too long ago, when two people of different races fell in love and wanted to live their lives together, society stopped them from symbolizing this by denying interracial marriage. That of course has changed. Today, if two people of the same sex fall in love, there are those who are fighting to deny their right to marry.

But people are people. Love is love. And marriage is marriage. Marriage is not easy but is worth fighting for, not against. Marriage requires letting go of individual autonomy, focusing on making the other person happy, being loyal and supportive, being patient and kind, and doing this over and over until death seems to separate us. I for one learned this again this week for the umpteenth time. I don't have to like my spouse's dog a lot, but because I love my spouse, I choose to be kind to the dog. And, I am learning to love her dog.

Who would not want this challenge and blessing for another human being? The sole purpose of marriage is not procreation. In fact, today, because Earth may be nearing its carrying capacity, marriages that cannot procreate may be a special blessing. And adoption is a great way to go; my wife and I adopted one of our two children, with very happy results.

Love will find a way. The problem is not that there is too much love and commitment in the world but that there is too little. Let's promote and enable love and lifelong commitment between people of any race, sexual orientation, religion, ethnicity, nationality, political persuasion, or class. Let wedding bells ring! And then happiness, struggle, and gratitude can flow forth and strengthen the larger community.

———

Peace and Nonviolence

Can I Be Like Malala?

In 2014, when I was in Nairobi consulting with UN Habitat, I wrote this reflection.

What is on my heart this Nairobi evening? I am thinking about the recent violence here at the Westgate Mall. Many people here are naturally still on edge—watchful, fearful. Before and after coming, I have been watchful, careful.

Then, Malala Yousafzai came to my mind—the amazing Pakistani girl-saint with a passion for education and peace. As many of us have read or heard, she said that if someone comes to attack her again, and if Malala has a gun, she would not shoot her attacker.

How can she say that? Doesn't she want to live? Doesn't she think her life is important? Certainly, her answer would be yes to both questions. Then how can she feel this way?

I think that she has decided deep in her heart to be a person who meets violence with nonviolence, fear with courage, and hatred with compassion. How did she learn this? How can she do this? Who is she? What is she?

My question tonight is, how can I be like Malala? How can I be a person of nonviolence, courage, and compassion?

What if there were millions of Malalas? What difference could it make to a world wracked with fear, anger, and hatred? Surely, it would make a world of difference.

———

How Can We Transform a Culture of Violence?

Violence is on my mind a lot these days. What do I have to say about violence? We are drowning in a national and global culture of violence. Where do I see that? I experience impulses toward violence within myself when I am hurt or angry. My national government launches billion-dollar acts of violence around the world at any provocation or without any provocation. Many men practice violence within their homes with their wives and children. Our police use massive violence against their own citizens. My country has more people in prison than does any other nation on Earth.

We are a leader in exporting military weapons around the world. We provide huge grants to other countries to support their military operations. We bomb other nations when we find something that we do not like. We invade sovereign nations at will. Our people carry more guns and kill more fellow and sister citizens than any other country. Our children are massacred in their classrooms. Our country has the largest military with the largest budget in the world.

Massive extraction of fossil fuels and carbon emissions of industrialized nations of the world, led by China and the United States, are destroying forests and species, poisoning drinking water, putting toxins into the air we breathe, acidifying the oceans, warming the planet, melting polar ice, causing catastrophic megastorms, damaging food production, and causing massive droughts and floods.

Unarmed black men are shot and killed because they are black. Video games, TV shows, and movies flood our eyes and minds with scenes of violence. CEOs are paid millions of dollars to put thousands of employees out of work in order to generate more profits for shareholders. Many people work a forty-hour workweek with such low wages that they cannot care for themselves and their families. A few nations, including my own, have huge arsenals of nuclear weapons. Many nations have nuclear power plants that can leak deadly radioactivity.

And on and on and on. I will not go on.

What are we to think about this predicament? What can we do about this madness?

How can we, on the other hand, create a culture of peace and justice?

First of all, I am sickened and weep over the suffering brought about by violence. I myself must become a person of peace and justice in my own heart, in my relationships, in my livelihood, in my work, in my voting, in my shopping, in my investing, and so on. I must create a peaceful and just family and a peaceful and just community. I must call my nation to the way of peace and justice. I must call humankind around this fair planet to a life of justice and peace. I must hold government and corporations accountable for acts of violence and demand that they promote peace and justice instead.

Instead of responding violently when we are fearful, angry, or hateful, let us as individuals and as a nation first practice listening, dialoguing, understanding, using diplomacy, negotiating, compromising, respecting, empathizing, and showing compassion. Yes, let us even attempt to relieve the suffering of our enemies. For if they are wedded to violence, are they not trapped in suffering and confusion? Yes, let's reach out beyond our armor, put aside our weaponry, and dare to be vulnerable—not in a stupid way but in a strategic and smart way.

But first, for me, I must calm my own negative emotions, my anger, my hatred, my pride, my fear, and my greed. I must practice peace in my thinking, doing, and being.

May it be so even now, even here.

9/11: Respond with Violence or Compassion?

This is my reflection on 9/11 as I arrived in New York City that morning.

That morning, I took the train as usual to Manhattan. In Grand Central Station, I noticed people gathered around a TV monitor in a bookstore. I stopped and saw pictures of smoke coming from one of the World Trade Center towers. The announcer said that it might have been a plane off course.

I walked to the UN building and took an elevator to my office's floor. A group of colleagues were gathered around a computer screen. They said that two planes had crashed into the Twin Towers and that the UN was being evacuated in case it was another target. I went into my office and cried, thinking of the people dying in the buildings and planes.

A colleague and I walked to a friend's apartment. From there, I could see smoke billowing from the Twin Towers far to the south. Because the apartment was across the street from the UN, we left and walked back to Grand Central Station. The streets were streaming with people walking north. There were crowds around the doors of Grand Central, with police monitoring the flow of people. Inside,

I found a train going to Fleetwood, just north of the city, where my youngest son lived.

My son picked me up and took me to his apartment. His girl-friend (now his wife) was there along with my wife and older son. They had just arrived after trying to get to Columbia Presbyterian Hospital for my wife's chemotherapy session and then learning of the attacks. Everyone was sober and quiet. I cried again and said that life would never be the same. I thought of who might have forced the planes to crash, and I wept for their confusion, anger, and hatred.

A few days later, I wrote several essays on the tragedy, recommending that the United States not respond in violence and hatred but with dialogue, compassion, and understanding. I proposed that a multibillion-dollar poverty-eradication global fund be established to help those in need whose despair might drive them to acts of violence. I was so deeply sad when my country attacked Afghanistan.

After thirteen years of my country's violent actions in Iraq and elsewhere, the world is in more confusion and chaos, with more fear, anger, and hatred. When will we learn? Responding to violence with violence only creates more violence. Responding to hatred with hatred only creates more hatred. We must cut the flow of cause and effect. We must be still and silent. We must listen. We must understand. We must forgive. We must offer acts of kindness and compassion to relieve others' suffering. We must stop people from harming other people.

Now with climate chaos in full swing, civilization itself may be in danger of collapse over the next few decades. How do we reinvent a world that works for everyone and honors the life support systems of planet Earth? We must practice cultural and religious tolerance and understanding. We must foster social and economic justice. We must create a compassionate civilization or suffer the consequences.

Nonviolence Is the Path

If studies are true, as they show, that we humans are naturally empathic and caring, how can we explain the amount of harm we do to each other? Negative emotions—fear, anger, hatred, pride, and greed—cloud our minds and hearts and move us to commit violent acts. But there is a way out. We can become aware of our negative emotions, stop the chain reaction toward violence, slow down our responses, and choose another path and expression. It is possible. We know how to do this, and we can practice diligently.

In this regard, deciding to live as a nonviolent person is the best protection. If this is our vow, our default position, it helps us recognize the triggers toward harmful action and enables us to choose alternative courses of action.

But nonviolence is not so easy. Self-protection and survival are also powerful forces. How do we care for ourselves and those we love while we guard against harming others? Vowing to be a person who does no harm is a powerful antidote.

We live in a culture of violence—of war, militarism, guns, terrorism, drones, sexism, and racism. The voices of hatred and violence are all around us and within us. How do we cultivate peace within and without?

We must actively seek out and create alternatives to violent responses to violent acts. We must continue to cultivate peace within our individual hearts, minds, and behavior, even as we help catalyze cultural transformation and systems change toward compassion, peace, and understanding. We can do better. We must do better if the human project is to survive and flourish.

But violence is not only among humans but also between humans and the natural world. We rape the land to extract fossil fuels and minerals. We fill the air we breathe with toxic gases. We poison the water we drink. We damage the genetic structure of the plants we eat. We devour other animals, without a second thought. We can do better. We must do better.

Let us take refuge in, among others, Malala Yousafzai, Mahatma Gandhi, and Martin Luther King Jr., true disciples of nonviolence and peace. Let us build societies that ensure dignity and safety to all people everywhere and to the entirety of the natural world. We can do this. We must find a way to be at peace within ourselves and with others.

———

Four Faces of War and Peace

The reflection below is excerpted from my speech to the Creative Peacemaking Symposium 2014 at Oklahoma City University.

May all people everywhere, including you and me, realize peace, happiness, understanding, and compassion.

A Cherokee prayer: "O Great Spirit, help me always to speak the truth quietly, to listen with an open mind when others speak, and to remember the peace that may be found in silence."

We are so busy, rushing about here and there. Let's begin by relaxing our body and bringing our mind to stillness and quiet. Please relax your body. Become aware of your body, breath, and mind. Take five minutes...

What did you notice or experience?

I grew up in Oklahoma and went to Oklahoma State University. I am proud that our state logo has two symbols of peace covering an Osage shield: the calumet, or peace pipe, representing Native Americans, and the olive branch, representing European Americans.

As you know, the UN is dedicated to peace and development. It is often said that there can be no peace without development and no development without peace. I have spent my life working on the development side so that we may have a lasting peace. Thus, I am a development expert, not a peace expert.

We live in a world at war. Peacemaking is the life-and-death vocation of our time. How are you called to use your creativity and energy?

Who is most concerned about climate chaos? Gender inequality? Socioeconomic injustice? Dysfunctional governance? Cultural intolerance?

Mind, Behavior, Culture, and Systems

War involves acts of violence and harm, whereas peace includes dialogue and justice. Ken Wilber's integral map can help us see the four faces of war and peace.

Take a few minutes and think about what is going on in each quadrant, both what you think is contributing to violence and harm or war in that particular dimension and what can promote dialogue and justice or peace. Share your ideas with someone. Below are a few of my thoughts about these four faces of war and peace, for your consideration:

Mind of Warmongering: A violent, harmful mind emerges as negative emotions arise from our confusion about our true nature of compassion and wisdom. When we separate ourselves from others, negative emotions of fear, anger, hatred, greed, and pride take root. These negative emotions can control our mind and then find expression in our behavior.

Mind of Peacemaking: We can cultivate a mind of peacemaking through meditating; empathizing; practicing ethics, compassion, and wisdom; moving beyond ego; experiencing unity; and manifesting generosity, equanimity, and trust. Exemplars of the mind of peacemaking include His Holiness the Fourteenth Dalai Lama. He says, "Many people today agree that we need to reduce violence in our society. If we are truly serious about this, we must deal with the roots of violence, particularly those that exist within each of us. We need to embrace 'inner disarmament,' reducing our own emotions of suspicion, hatred, and hostility toward our brothers and sisters." Methods of fostering a mind of peacemaking include meditation and ethical practice. But this is never easy. Where do you struggle with letting go of negative emotions?

Behavior of Warmongering: Violent, harmful behaviors include acts of superiority or hatred toward other races, women, or different sexual and gender orientations, as well as greed, consumerism, corruption, meat-eating, being part of a throwaway society, and carrying a gun.

Behavior of Peacemaking: We can cultivate the behavior of peacemaking through practicing happiness, nonviolence, facilitative leadership, collaboration, compassionate action, reconciliation, mediation, and vegetarianism; promoting diversity; and caring for environmental sustainability. Exemplars of the behavior of peacemaking include Martin Luther King Jr., Mahatma Gandhi, and Peace Pilgrim, who walked across America for twenty-eight years. Malala has said, "I would not shoot someone threatening me." Methods of behavioral peacemaking include nonviolent resistance and group facilitation. But this is never easy. How do you struggle to manage your harmful behavior?

Culture of Warmongering: Violent, harmful cultures emerge from stories, symbols, and rituals of racism, sexism, intolerance, nationalism, classism, ageism, and homophobia.

Culture of Peacemaking: We can catalyze a culture of peacemaking by living by principles of sustainability, justice, equality, participation, and tolerance. We can create new stories, songs, symbols, and rites that embody these principles. This year (2014) on March 1, a Climate March began to traverse the United States, which included my colleague David Zahrt along with many others. But it is never easy to manifest new cultural forms such as this high ritual. Where do you struggle to do this?

Systems of Warmongering: Violent, harmful systems are manifestations of collective greed, fear, anger, hatred, or pride, including practicing exorbitant wealth accumulation, militarism, and armed conflict; maintaining armed forces, the armaments industry, nuclear proliferation, and capital punishment; extracting, selling, and burning fossil fuels; honoring plutocracy; and allowing systemic poverty, injustice, and inequality.

Systems of Peacemaking: We can cultivate new systems of peacemaking by creating policies and institutions that promote environmental sustainability, renewable energy, socioeconomic justice, gender equality, participatory governance, cultural tolerance, nuclear disarmament, an end to capital punishment, delegitimized war, and universal education and health care. Exemplars of creating systems of peacemaking include Nelson Mandela and Bill McKibben of 350. org. But none of this is easy. Where do you struggle to challenge the present corrupt systems and catalyze new systems of justice?

Creative peacemaking can begin in any of the four quadrants. We can teach meditation, practice nonviolent networking, or advocate new stories or new policies. Wherever we begin, we can affect the other quadrants. We can also design projects that activate all four quadrants.

Most of us can agree with these faces of peacemaking. But what is blocking us? What is keeping this from happening? What do we need to do in order to do this? I struggle to do these things. What are your struggles? We need a balance between patience and consideration and between urgency and boldness. How can we do this? It isn't easy. It is very challenging. It can be boring. It is hard work. Its outcome is uncertain. It won't make us rich or popular. How do we move forward day after day?

Who is drawn to help nurture the mind of peacemaking? The behavior of peacemaking? The culture of peacemaking? Systems and policies of peacemaking? All four dimensions?

Strategies, Partnerships, and Projects

We can design creative initiatives and projects of education, networking, and advocacy.

Education: We can design educational projects to promote creative peacemaking. These can involve teaching meditation or ethics and providing relevant information. They can teach nonviolent resistance, facilitation, mediation, new stories of dialogue and justice, and new policy messages.

Networking: We can design networking projects that promote collaboration and group facilitation. We can promote networking among diverse communities to nurture understanding, among facilitators and mediators, among new exemplars of peacemaking, and among policy makers.

Advocacy: We can also design projects that advocate for new mindsets, individual behaviors, new cultural expressions, or new policies and institutions of peacemaking. These can involve speaking out, writing, blogging, creating art forms, and engaging in politics.

We can invent creative new pathways to peace: new language, new methods, new partnerships, new projects, new ideas, new rituals, and new policies.

My challenge to you is to push for breakthrough-thinking toward radical being and doing. Speak your truth. Listen to each other's truth. Risk bold proposals. Manifest your ground of values. Dare to be the change that the world needs. These are the times. And we are the people!

May all people everywhere, including you and me, realize peace, happiness, understanding, and compassion.

"Ain't Gonna Study War No More"
(from the song "Down By the Riverside")

The following are a few minireflections on the end of warfare.

- Our spiritual teachers say "Do not kill," "Turn the other cheek," "Love your enemy," "Relieve others' suffering," and "Nonviolence is the only way." Yet we ignore their wisdom and continue killing, hating, and reacting to violence with violence.
- There are alternatives to war, including dialogue, negotiation, diplomacy, economic sanctions, UN resolutions and peace-keeping, nonviolent resistance, forgiveness, global shaming, economic assistance, pacifism, protecting the innocent, indirection, distraction, removal from danger, and self-sacrifice.
- War is nationally sanctioned mass murder, immoral, and an abomination that brutalizes and traumatizes everyone.

- War has been tragically romanticized to appeal to a young man's self-image as warrior and hero.
- The technologies of war make it appear to be a life-size video game. It is not. It is real blood, real suffering, and real death.
- Nations call their young into harm's way. Yet if their young return home, they are not supported with adequate health and employment opportunities and often end up poor, sick, and suicidal.
- Only one nation has ever dropped atomic bombs on innocent civilians. On behalf of my beloved country, I express limitless sorrow and regret and vow, "Never again."
- War is mass insanity. No other species engages in war to the extent we do. It is a uniquely human disease.
- There is no such thing as a "just" war. All war is unjust and criminal. Wars are a collective expression of delusion, greed, fear, anger, and hatred.
- Wars will stop when people refuse to kill other people.
- Every human being desires happiness, love, peace, health, respect, a long life, and friendship.

War Is Terrorism

The Delegitimating of War

The images coming out of Iraq a few years ago made me sick in my stomach and in my heart. The following is my reflection on these atrocities.

War is hell. Why then are we shocked when we see images of cruelty and violence? This is the very nature of war. We confuse our young sons and daughters by sending them out with national approbation to kill and maim other people's young sons and daughters, and then we are horrified when they treat their prisoners cruelly. Is it better to kill someone or to abuse them? Neither is better. Both are horrible. War traumatizes us all, violates us all. Yet some people find something perversely scintillating about seeing someone being abused. Harming others brings out the very worst in us all.

The entire enterprise of war is illegitimate. As long as there are parents who send their young sons and daughters into this hell, and as long as these young men and women obey their parents and their government, the illegitimacy and horror will continue to retain the illusion of legitimacy and rationality.

There must be a better way of resolving human disagreements.

There is a grander vision of human development that can displace the warrior's thrill of conquest and sacrifice. We now have global and regional institutions to help resolve conflicts. People universally desire happiness and peace for themselves and their families. The time is fast approaching when it will be agreed that war, like slavery, is an abomination of humankind and will not be tolerated anymore.

War Is Terrorism

Terrorism mistranslated as "war"
Although war has always brought terror

Barbarism, a primitive instinct
Of the human animal
Or more precisely, of the
Male ego—warrior and killer, driven by
Hormones and emotion and the
Comradeship of other males
Dying for that which is greater
Uniting with the Great Cause
Becoming one with Life and Death
A tragically flawed mysticism
And for what?
Oil? Democracy? Disarmament? Freedom?
Righteousness? Empire? Corporate contracts?
Such heartbreak
To see our precious, soft
Baby boys and girls grow up to
Maim and kill other babies, women, men
Who were once soft and precious
Held in their mothers' arms
Now cold and hard
And to be maimed or die themselves
May our hearts grow ever larger to give space to
Everyone
May a mother's love rise within
Each of us
May we tame and transcend our egos
May we give up war for

Wisdom

And carnage for

Compassion

———

Paris: Love, Light, or Terror?

I felt horror and sadness at the shocking deaths of those who died in the attacks in Paris. I grieved with their families and friends. As the airwaves filled with reflections about terrorism and what to do about it, I wrote a few of my thoughts.

Terrorism depends on your point of view. For example, when the American revolutionaries were burning English churches, they were seen as terrorists by the English and as patriots by those wishing separation from the Crown. Who was right? If the revolution had been put down, the "patriots" would be terrorists to this day.

Terrorism can be effective only if those toward whom it is directed feel terrorized, and that depends entirely on them. How we respond to tragedy is up to each of us. For example, after twenty young men took down the Twin Towers in 2001 and three thousand people were killed, the mood in New York City and around the world was universal shock, sadness, and even a welling up of a sense of the preciousness of life and its interdependence. Only later did the US government and the mass media help turn that into fear, anger, hatred, and retaliation by launching an endless "war on terror" that itself became endless terrorism. There were other responses possible.

Terrorists win if their enemies respond with institutionalized fear and violence. The US government created Homeland Security, a multibillion-dollar agency, and spent trillions of taxpayer and borrowed dollars attacking Afghanistan and then Iraq, which had nothing to do with 9/11. We have gone into massive debt, lost or traumatized thousands of our citizens in battle, and given birth to ISIS. Who is winning the war on terror?

Terrorism arises because people feel powerless, disrespected, threatened, unseen, and unheard. They then decide that their only option is to attack the evil system that is harming them and threatening their beliefs and way of life. Religiously motivated terrorists—whether Christian, Muslim, or whatever—are some of the most zealous because they each believe that God is on their side and that they must destroy unbelievers. They are all equally mistaken, however, and should not be allowed to attack each other and draw others into their fanaticism of fear and hatred.

What are nonviolent options of the dominant system in responding to minority fears, anger, and violence? The dominant system must engage in deep reflection by asking itself several questions at this point: What is it in our behavior that has provoked such a violent response? What are the legitimate concerns of those who are responding in violence? How can dialogue take place that allows every party to express their concerns, fears, and hopes? What options are available that honor everyone's views and allow for a common nonviolent solution? The dominant system must be willing to make changes, compromises, and adjustments in behavior and policy. Needless to say, it is essential for the dominant system to do all that it can to protect the safety and well-being of all citizens during this process.

What are responses that the dominant system must be careful to avoid in the midst of terrorist acts? Demonizing larger groups must be avoided. If the person who bombed the federal building in Oklahoma City is a Christian, all Christians must not be demonized. If the attackers in Paris were Muslim, all Muslims must not be demonized. Exacerbating fear among the general population must be avoided. There must be voices of calm and reason during the mourning period that remind people to focus on living their daily lives in confidence and gratitude, reaching out to minority groups and disaffected people.

At times like these, we must remember even greater threats to our shared humanity, such as continuing environmental degradation and climate chaos; growing oligarchy and militarism; and increasing human misery through systemic poverty, gender violence, cultural intolerance, and nuclear arms proliferation. How do we reinvent our societies and move toward a compassionate civilization for all?

There are no easy answers or magic solutions. We must do all that we can to listen to others, to look within our own hearts, and be willing to risk the status quo by creating something new out of the confrontation of differences. We must see that a common solution will be one that allows everyone to be who they are without doing harm to others.

———

PART 2

WHO WILL CATALYZE A COMPASSIONATE CIVILIZATION, HOW WILL THEY LEAD, AND HOW WILL THEY CARE FOR THEMSELVES AND OTHERS?

CHAPTER 4

THE MOVEMENT OF MOVEMENTS (MOM)

How will we get from our current situation of crisis to a new civilization of compassion? Fortunately, there are already several forces moving us in that direction. These are the many movements that each promote a particular vision. If they can work together, these movements will become a powerful "movement of movements" that will help humanity realize its full potential.

How Will the MOM Save Us?

One person acts out of conscience and passion, then another. They form an organization to accomplish their mission of making a better world. Their organization links up with other similar organizations. Then, many such organizations come together to form a movement. Finally, several movements join forces to form a movement of movements (MOM), a network of networks. This is the way it works by the laws of attraction and cooperation, a groundswell of good intentions and compassionate actions.

Take the natural environment. There are many powerful organizations at work with different founders and approaches. Greenpeace, 350.org, and Transition Towns are three of them. How do these three, along with hundreds of other similar organizations, share knowledge and strategies, join forces, and engage in cooperative activism to form a movement for sustainable environment and climate chaos mitigation and adaptation?

How then does this movement link up with movements committed to other societal goals, including gender equality, participatory governance, campaign finance reform, human rights, fiscal reform, universal health, stopping the sex trade, education for all, job creation, cultural and religious tolerance, disarmament and peace, and so on, to manifest in a MOM?

MOM should be light and networked. No need for more legal entities, buildings, meetings, committees, and CEOs. MOM needs websites, apps, chat rooms, LISTSERVs, Facebook pages, Twitter feeds, LinkedIn pages, Trusted Sharing conversations, shared blog posts, joint training events and rallies, cooperative projects, common lobbyists, orchestrated mass media releases, synergistic talking heads, get-out-the-vote campaigns, mass boycotts, strategic fund raising, e-newsletters, e-journals, and more.

A Sampling of the MOM

Environmental, Climate, and Green Energy Movements: The environmental movement is committed to protecting the natural environment. The climate movement is motivated to help us mitigate and adapt to climate chaos. The green energy movement is promoting the rapid transition to an energy system of 100 percent renewable energy from the sun, wind, water, geothermal sources, and algae.

This includes networks and organizations such as just mentioned, 350.org, Greenpeace, and Transition Towns.

Women's and LGBTQ Movements: The women's movement promotes the rights, voice, leadership, and protection of women. Women gained the right to vote in the US only ninety-five years ago, and they must be paid the same as men for the same work. The LGBTQ movement is concerned about the safety and freedom of lesbian, gay, bisexual, transgender, and queer youth and adults. Groups in these movements include the National Organization of Women (NOW) and International Gay and Lesbian Human Rights Commission and others.

Direct Democracy and Decentralization Movements: The direct democracy movement promotes the formation of new democratic processes and institutions that allow the views and needs of citizens to be the basis for policy formulation. Three important signs of hope in the United States are Indivisible Guide, Democracy Spring, and Our Revolution. The decentralization movement helps move power, decision-making, and service delivery beyond national and state capitals to towns and villages throughout a country. Cities and associations of local authorities are often more progressive than their national governments.

Labor Union and Transformed-Capitalism Movements: The labor movement helps workers organize into unions that can negotiate their salaries and benefits so that they are not taken advantage of by management. Workers must be paid a living wage. The transformed-capitalism movement is promoting the creation of a new economic system that values the well-being of all the people and all of nature over profits for a small elite. Recent books by Robert Reich and Naomi Klein clarify that we need a capitalism for the many, not the few, and we must change the form of capitalism that is endangering life on Earth through climate change.

Human Rights and Peace Movements: The human rights movement is committed to realizing the Universal Declaration of Human Rights for every woman, man, and child. The peace movement is working hard to promote nonviolence, diplomacy, and negotiation; to stop wars; and to delegitimize war as an acceptable manner for resolving conflict.

Group Facilitation and Social Artistry Movements: The facilitation movement is promoting the power of group facilitation as a way to involve all the people of an organization or community in its own decision-making. This includes the International Association of Facilitators (IAF) and the ToP Network (the Technology of Participation Network), created by the Institute of Cultural Affairs (ICA). Every year, International Facilitation Week celebrates the power of group facilitation. The social artistry movement trains educators and leaders in organizations and communities to enhance people's creativity and passion in ways that create a world that works for all. This includes the work of the Jean Houston Foundation.

Of course there are many other movements as well. The point is that when these movements work together, they are unstoppable. They can and will create a new civilization of compassion. The UN is among those at the forefront of this MOM. One hundred and ninety-three member states of the UN launched seventeen Sustainable Development Goals (SDGs) for 2030 (see annex.) Achieving these goals will take us a long way toward a new civilization of compassion.

Which movement is your favorite? Which one are you already part of? Which one do you want to become part of? Please visit this book's bibliography for websites of many of the above organizations.

• • •

In the next chapter, we will explore some of the most powerful leadership approaches that each individual leader, organization, or movement or the MOM can utilize in catalyzing a compassionate civilization.

Let's hear it for MOM! May a compassionate civilization rise up in our midst, moment by moment.

.

CHAPTER 5

INNOVATIVE LEADERSHIP APPROACHES

Today, the dominant style of leadership is command-and-control. The leader is seen as superior and to be obeyed and is usually male. Leadership is seen to be about strength, authority, and control of others. One of the problems with this approach to leadership is that it does not seek or value the views, intelligence, and participation of other people. It is therefore less intelligent and does not reflect the ideas and needs of other people and causes them harm.

A compassionate civilization will be created through and embody innovative leadership. Leadership will have evolved beyond the authoritative, bureaucratic, and pragmatic to principled and system-wide leadership honoring multiple perspectives. Leadership will be understood as an art of human behavior and interaction that can be practiced by anyone in any position. Leadership will be facilitative, participatory, inspiring, systemic, and creative.

Integral, Facilitative, Social Artistry, and Mindful Leadership

To move from our time of crisis toward a new civilization of compassion, we need to provide innovative leadership of the movement of movements and in governments, corporations, nongovernment organizations (NGOs), academia, and media. There are many methods of effective and innovative leadership. I would like to share four that I have found to be particularly powerful: (1) integral systems thinking, (2) group facilitation and participatory planning, (3) social artistry, and (4) mindfulness, ethics, and servant-leadership.

Integral Systems Thinking (Four Quadrants)

The innovative leader engages in integral systems thinking in four dimensions based on Ken Wilber's integral quadrants—the interior (consciousness) and exterior (the material world) and the individual and collective. By analyzing and planning within four quadrants at the intersection of these dimensions, the innovative leader is aware of and is addressing all aspects of any issue or situation. She knows that every situation has an interior-individual dimension, an exterior-individual dimension, an interior-collective dimension, and an exterior-collective dimension. The interior-individual dimension includes people's mind-sets, attitudes, values, and assumptions, which as a leader you must be aware of and help evolve. The exterior-individual dimension includes people's behaviors, speech, and interpersonal relations that need new skillful means. The interior-collective dimension includes culture, myths, symbols, rituals, and norms that influence people, some of which need to be transformed. The exterior-collective dimension includes systems, policies, institutions, organizations, and communities that need to evolve continually. For example, in dealing with climate change, the innovative leader must employ strategies to change individual mind-sets and behavior, as well as collective culture and systems. When I was at the UN, I used integral systems thinking to help design new policies and programs. (For more information, contact the Integral Institute at in.integralinstitute.org/integral.aspx)

Group Facilitation and Participatory Planning (ToP)

The innovative leader uses group facilitation techniques and processes to enable people to engage in participatory conversations and planning. The facilitator asks question after question to provoke the best thinking and cooperation of the group. For example, in the Technology of Participation (ToP) methodology, created by the Institute of Cultural Affairs (ICA), the innovative leader facilitates group conversations in a four-part sequence called ORID: **O**bjective, **R**eflective, **I**nterpretive, and **D**ecisional. This allows the group to go from an objective appreciation ("What do you notice?"), to delving into their emotions and memory ("How do you feel about it?" or "What does it remind you of?"), to telling a story or identifying the meaning ("What is the significance?"), and finally to making a decision concerning what actions are needed ("What is your decision?"). In the ToP strategic planning process, the facilitator leads the group to (1) articulate their practical vision, (2) analyze underlying obstacles to the vision, (3) create strategic directions to deal with the obstacles and move toward the vision, and (4) decide on an action plan for realizing the strategies. I often facilitate online conversations on the Trusted Sharing platform using the ORID method. When I was in the UNDP, I used the participatory strategic planning method to develop policies and projects around the world. (For further information, you may contact the Institute of Cultural Affairs at www.ica-international.org)

Social Artistry

The innovative leader uses social-artistry techniques and processes developed by Dr. Jean Houston to enhance people's creativity and commitment. The social artist enables people to become aware of and involved in social change on four levels: sensory/physical, psychological/historical, mythic/symbolic, and unitive/integral. At the sensory/physical level, people deepen their awareness of the physical situation using their five senses. At the psychological/historical level, people look at their memories, feelings, and associations. At the mythic/symbolic level, people explore the stories and symbols that give meaning to their lives, and they also create new stories concerning new possibilities. And at the unitive/integral level, people experience the sense of unity or oneness with the group or reality that they are dealing with. If the social artist can expand and deepen people's awareness on these four levels, there is greater likelihood of achieving creative, inspiring, and lasting change. When I was in the UNDP, I was involved in training people in several countries in social artistry so that they could be more effective in decentralizing the Millennium Development Goals and, later, the Sustainable Development Goals in their countries by enhancing their human capacities. (To explore and learn further, contact the Jean Houston Foundation at www.jeanhouston.org/social-artistry/social-artistry.html)

Mindfulness, Ethics, and Servant-Leadership

The innovative leader uses mindfulness exercises and ethical practices to call people to a profound sense of being servant-leaders. Mindfulness exercises include relaxation, meditation, contemplation, and yoga. By enhancing and deepening their awareness, people gain detached engagement, understanding, compassion, and wisdom. Ethical study and practice help people live lives based on their deepest values and principles, such as compassion, truth, justice, equality, and understanding. Learning to be a servant-leader is a lifelong journey of letting go of one's ego and focusing one's energies on helping and serving others. I meditate daily and teach my NYU grad students all four of the above leadership methods.

These four approaches to innovative leadership, among others, are needed to propel organizations, movements, and the movement of movements toward the realization of a compassionate civilization. These innovative leadership methods can be learned, practiced, and applied in organizations, communities, and whole societies.

Let's shock the world with compassionate, sustainable development for all!

Collaborative, Engaged, and Transformative Leadership

Collaborative Leadership: A Necessity

The following are excerpts from my presentation on collaborative leadership at the 2014 UN Public Service Global Forum on Sustainable Development held in Seoul, Korea.

We can commit ourselves to collaborative action to create a healthy planetary ecosystem, gender equality, socioeconomic justice, participatory governance, and cultural tolerance. Innovative solutions and actions are urgently needed at every level of government, industry, and civil society to respond to these multiple, interlocking crises. To achieve innovative solutions and effective actions, new kinds of collaboration among these three governance actors are needed, as well as collaboration among government agencies themselves, among NGOs, among corporations, and among the individuals within each of these.

Earlier this year, I taught a seminar on collaborative leadership at the University of Aruba with Dr. Juliet Chieuw. Suddenly, I became aware that the major challenge of collaboration is that *it involves other people*! Working with other people is never easy but is essential to the success of the human enterprise. Let's briefly explore the concepts and practice of collaboration, leadership, methods of collaborative leadership, and how it is essential to our survival as a species.

What is collaboration? Collaboration involves engaging in teamwork; promoting synergy; and creating collective intelligence, mutual respect, trust, and learning. It involves honoring diverse perspectives and gifts, moving beyond one's own ego, achieving a common vision, and acknowledging values and self-organization. One of my favorite examples of this is within the private sector. To invent the Visa card, Dee Hock had a group of diverse individuals work together with only two things in common: a shared vision and shared values. Out of their collaboration emerged the design of the Visa card based on the collaboration of competing businesses that were committed to using the Visa card for business transactions.

And as for us, I believe our common vision is sustainable human development or what I have identified as an emerging civilization of compassion. And I believe that our common values include not only sustainability but also equality, justice, participation, and tolerance. But we must invite everyone to participate in this brainstorming on vision and values.

What is leadership? Leadership has developmental phases, including the authoritative, the bureaucratic, and the pragmatic. It can also evolve into participatory, facilitative, creative, system-wide, interactive, adaptive, and transformative leadership. Group facilitation is a great example of this new style of leadership. In this form of leadership, the facilitator asks question after question to help a group of people identify their shared visions, obstacles, strategies, and action plans. By honoring individual brainstorming, collective grouping of data, and naming of clusters of data, a group of people can collaborate in creating a strategic plan that they own because they created it. And they are motivated to carry out the plan because it is their own, as individuals and as a group. In this workshop, we are using participatory methods that allow everyone in the room to create recommended actions for member states and the UN.

What then is collaborative leadership? Collaborative leadership is a dynamic, creative, self-organizing team of orchestrated, diverse perspectives and gifts driven by common vision and values. To launch a rocket into space, many technicians must collaborate intimately. The entire enterprise of science requires careful collaboration among many scientists around the globe. A choreographer must collaborate with individual dancers to produce a great work of art. Architects of communal spaces must collaborate with the public to design workable solutions. Within whole-of-government, collaborative leadership is the commitment to honoring every individual and every agency's insights and knowledge in the creation of open, transparent, and accountable governance systems responsive to the voices and priorities of every citizen, especially the most vulnerable.

Why then is collaborative leadership essential in a whole-of-government approach?

This critical moment of history requires everyone's participation and collaboration. How otherwise can nations and communities respond to the multiple crises we face without effective collaboration? Everyone's perspective and energy in every government agency is needed in a concerted effort. Every NGO and business must be involved. And all of these must be working harmoniously together in a common cause. Finally, the intelligence and energy of 7.3 billion people must be mobilized and orchestrated with common vision and values in seamless action.

What are some of the most effective methods and applications of collaborative leadership? The most effective methods of collaborative leadership that I am aware of include group facilitation (such as the ToP, Appreciative Inquiry, and Open Space); the use of integral frameworks addressing individual mind-sets and behaviors and collective cultures and institutions; social artistry processes that enhance sensory, psychological, symbolic, and unitive experience; systems thinking; strategic planning; effective team building; and peer learning-by-doing.

Collaboration is not only worth the effort; it has become a necessity if we humans are to enjoy sustainable human development on a healthy planet.

———

Catalyzing Empathic, Engaged Citizens

The following are excerpts from a presentation on citizens' leadership that I made at the UN Public Service Forum in New York City on June 26, 2012.

Citizen Engagement

Around the world, citizens are arising with new energy for transformation. The Arab Spring and the Occupy Wall Street movements were two manifestations of this. People are demanding that they participate and lead in their own governance and development. It is time to move beyond the control of corporatocracy, plutocracy, oligarchy, patriarchy, and militarism. Citizens are capable of governing their societies through their own intelligence, voice, and energy.

Education, health care, justice, livelihood, shelter, food, water, and sanitation are universal human rights and services that can be provided for all, to all, and by all. Current policies based on scarcity must be replaced by policies of sufficiency and sharing.

Citizens everywhere have organized as NGOs and community-based organizations (CBOs) to engage in self-governance and development. Civil society as a whole is now seen clearly as one of the three governance actors, the other two being government and the private sector. The environmental movement, the women's movement, and the human rights movement are the direct voices of citizens to create a sustainable and human world. To empower these citizen movements, new and effective institutional and leadership capacities are needed.

We see around the world NGOs and CBOs collaborating with local authorities and local businesses to improve the living environment in low-income settlements. We see NGOs and CBOs improving sanitation systems and waste management, providing clean drinking water, and starting clinics and community schools. We see NGOs and CBOs speaking out for the rights of the poor, minorities, women, youth, and the elderly. We see NGOs giving voice on behalf of other species, the oceans, air, and soil. People everywhere are waking up to their interconnectedness through social media, mass media, and travel and know their rights and their power to direct the course of history.

Knowledgeable, engaged citizens—of communities, nations, and the globe—are the keys to confronting the overwhelming challenges facing us and creating a new, empathic civilization of sustainable human development.

Innovative Leadership

No longer can leadership be by command-and-control. Absolute authority doesn't work and is inappropriate for a race of intelligent, creative beings. Local and national governments are being called to a new style of leadership to empower and engage citizens in their own governance and development. The leadership needed at this time of crisis and opportunity must be integral, facilitative, and creative.

Traditionally, change processes have focused exclusively on institutional arrangements, policies, and systems. This collective-exterior leadership is critical but is not sufficient. Change must also happen within the culture itself—the collective interior—by changing collective values and norms through motivating and transformative stories, rites, and symbols. Change must happen in individual values and behavior—the individual interior and individual exterior dimensions—changing mind-sets and perspectives, as well as relational and interpersonal behavior. This is integral leadership—working to change collective institutions and culture and individual mind-sets and behavior. In addition to having the right legal frameworks in place, we must have the right individual and collective values and behaviors moving our societies toward a more sustainable and human future.

The facilitative leader sees himself as a guide who enables groups of people to think, analyze, plan, and act together through participatory, interactive processes. The facilitative leader asks questions of people that allow them to journey together in a structured manner toward productive outcomes. Facilitation of citizen participation is essential to motivate and call forth the creativity and energy of all the people to respond to the massive challenges facing us today. Facilitation can be learned as a new type of leadership that does not control outcomes but provides participatory processes that allow citizens to create the policies and services that are most important to them.

Facilitation requires skill and patience, an ability to listen deeply, and willingness to allow citizens to chart pathways of good governance and effective development. The facilitative leader has the skill to lead productive discussions, analytical and problem-solving workshops, strategic planning exercises, and whole system design processes. The facilitative leader asks people to articulate their hoped-for vision of the future; the factors that could enable or inhibit reaching that vision; and the strategic directions that would carry them toward their vision, taking into account the inhibiting and enhancing factors and the implementation action plan and timeline that they will commit to in the day-to-day.

The government and NGOs must provide a multitude of opportunities of facilitated citizen dialogue and decision-making through forums, workshops, conferences, online chat rooms, websites, and social media.

The creative leader is a social artist who awakens and enlivens people's capacities in the dimensions of the sensory/physical, psychological/historical, mythic/symbolic, and unitive/spiritual. The creative leader provides processes by which people can access their own creativity, intuition, motivation, courage, vision, and genius in solving problems and designing new systems. The leader as social artist enables citizens to deepen their capacities of body, mind, and spirit in order to release their full potential as human beings. The creative leader makes use of individual and group processes, both face to face and online, that stimulate the best thinking, doing, and being in others that is possible.

The integral, facilitative, and creative leaders help turn challenges into opportunities for sustainable human development. The government and NGO officials who learn and practice these skills find themselves becoming true civil servants—the servants of the people—which they have pledged to be as elected or appointed leaders.

Conclusion

We can practice facilitative, creative, and integral leadership as we share our knowledge with each other and make recommendations for ourselves, each of the member states, and the United Nations as a whole. We can listen deeply for insights in presentations and discussions. As poet Rainer Maria Rilke says, we can "live the questions." We can be the People of the Question. We can ask "What if?" and act as if it were possible. We can become an emerging community of practice on governance and development.

Related to the concept of gross national happiness, happiness will not be our goal but our way of being as we catalyze well-being for ourselves and all others. A sense of hope will carry us through this tumultuous time of crisis and danger, and the lure of a possible future will draw us toward it—a new, empathic civilization of sustainable human development. Innovative leaders within government and throughout our societies are needed to help humanity through this great transition. If not us, whom? If not now, when?

———

Transformative Civilizational Leadership

The following is an excerpt from my plenary presentation to six hundred participants from around the world attending the UN and Africa Public Service Forum held in Dar es Salaam, Tanzania, on June 20, 2011.

Jambo! Habari?

I am very happy to be with you. Why are we here—in Africa, in this gathering? I have returned to Mother Africa, East Africa, as a pilgrim to the birthplace of the human species. I am part of this gathering because I am convinced that you and I can make a difference in this glorious, suffering world by what we think, say, and do.

In the midst of this critical decade, we must build a new civilization of sustainable human development, country by country, organization by organization, community by community.

We are here together to celebrate successes and challenge ourselves to create a new civilization, lesson by lesson, story by story. We are here to advance that noble cause. Public service in the twenty-first century faces many challenges and opportunities. In the midst of the breaking down of an old civilization and the emergence of a new civilization, public service is now called more than ever before to provide innovative leadership for sustainable human development.

There are many styles of leadership that follow a developmental progression identified by Dennis Emberling. First, leadership can be authoritarian, exploitative, and coercive with the leader as the boss, dictator, or employer. Next, leadership can be bureaucratic with the focus on rules and roles with the leader as a manager, administrator, or "parent." The third stage of leadership is pragmatic with a focus on results with the leader as a guide. Next, leadership can be based on values and principles with the leader as a facilitator, coordinator, or coach. And finally, leadership can be systems based with a concern for multiple perspectives with no managers but true delegation of responsibility to all members of the team.

What, then, are the most effective means in this critical decade with which to build a new civilization? **Transformative leadership** approaches are keys to unlock our human potential.

Transformative leadership methods will help us catalyze a new civilization in this critical decade through public service, public administration, and governance. If a leader makes use of these types of innovative methods, whole organizations, institutions, and communities will begin to mirror and emulate the leader's own awareness and prowess creating a powerful multiplying effect throughout the society. Can you imagine the use of transformative leadership approaches in a cabinet meeting, a parliament, a civil service bureaucracy, a corporate board room, or an NGO meeting and what a difference they could make?

Transformative leadership moves a society from a past-oriented problem-solving mode to a future-oriented whole systems design mode. It helps transform individual mind-sets, values, and behavior, as well as collective culture and institutions. The transformative leader is deeply concerned and committed to creating the conditions in a society that enable each woman, man, and child to realize her or his full potential. Transformative leadership makes use of participatory, interactive methods to ensure that each person's voice and wisdom is heard and felt in social dialogue and policy-making. The transformative leader is a social artist who makes use of myths, stories, rituals, symbols, and metaphors to motivate the society to imagine and reach its future vision.

Transformative leadership makes use of the very latest information technologies to enable the population to participate in governance processes at every level. The transformative leader is a person of deep personal integrity and empathy who manifests compassion for other people. He or she is committed to being the servant of the people in helping everyone live well. Transformative leadership is responsive to present and potential dangers and disasters and helps prepare and engage the population in doing what is needed to avert and deal with natural disasters, such as climate chaos, and human-made suffering, such as armed conflict. The transformative leader has a profound belief in universal human rights and is a powerful advocate for the empowerment of women, minorities, elders, and youth.

Transformative leadership works to create strong, accountable, and transparent democratic institutions and processes of governance. The transformative leader does everything in her power to help make a better life for all the people. In order to do this, she spends over half of her time managing her own ego, pride, greed, fear, anger, and hatred and practices concern for and understanding toward all people.

Following this forum, we the participants will return to our countries, organizations, and communities with renewed vision and practical tools for the betterment of our societies. We will stay networked electronically and will continue to challenge and encourage each other. We will make use of new methods of leadership and will help create new institutions of participatory governance. We will design new systems and structures, as well as new policies, programs, and projects that will put into practice the insights gained in the forum. We will continue to transform our own consciousness, values, and behavior as we help others transform theirs. We will catalyze new cultures of mutual respect and understanding among all people everywhere.

What if these four days in Dar marked a turning point in human history—from despair to hope, from greed to compassion, from impoverishment to empowerment? What if we the participants are indeed the people whom the world has been waiting for? What if we are the catalysts and servants whom history requires at this time? What if we are able to mobilize people in such a way as to respond to climate chaos, increasing poverty, dysfunctional governance, the HIV/AIDS pandemic, gender inequality, and economic collapse? What if we embody integrity, creativity, effectiveness, accountability, and transparency in everything we say and do?

What if we are the transformative leaders who call our fellow and sister citizens to join us in the greatest and noblest of tasks— to build Earth—to create a new civilization—to catalyze sustainable human development? What if these are indeed the times and we are indeed the people? What if we have come to East Africa to be reborn as truly *human* beings?

Asante sana!

———

Inspirational, Prophetic, and Systemic Leadership

Who or What Inspires You?

Where do you find inspiration these days? There is plenty going on in the world to concern us, sadden us, and frighten us. But what or who fills us or at least touches us with hope and inspiration? Actually, there are many people and activities that can inspire us.

Young and old activists around the world inspire us daily with their courage and passion for sustainability and justice. Whether it is Greenpeace activists risking their lives in the Arctic or 350.org activists protesting the Keystone Pipeline, we are given tangible hope that we can make a difference and turn the tide toward a better world for all.

Pope Francis is certainly saying and doing some surprising, inspiring things, yes? He seems genuinely to be in support of the least, the lost, and the last. He is calling out the global capitalist system for what it is—greedy, unjust, and harmful to people and planet. He is calling for tolerance and understanding among different lifestyle choices.

My colleagues inspire me with their commitment to sustainable human development, the work of the UN, the methods of the Institute of Cultural Affairs (ICA), the work of my NYU grad students, equality, justice, service to the poor, women's empowerment, teaching, political activism, care for the homeless, social artistry, group facilitation, and spiritual awakening.

His Holiness the Dalai Lama continues to be a deep source of inspiration for many. His commitment to living a life of compassion and understanding seems boundless. He genuinely wants people to be happy and kind. His humility and good humor are inspiring for sure.

Elizabeth Warren and Bernie Sanders both inspire me a lot with their clarity and passion for equality and justice. Jean Houston inspires me with her belief in the possibility and practice of releasing human potential. Hazel Henderson inspires me with her work tracking green energy investments. Bill McKibben inspires me with his total devotion to awakening people concerning climate chaos mitigation.

President Obama continues to inspire many people. In the midst of huge problems at home and abroad, his authenticity, likeability, and straight talk are refreshing. We are inspired by his persistent commitment to improving the lives of middle- and low-income citizens. Even when we don't agree with some of his administration's policies, such as the use of drones, there is something inspiring about his humanity.

After a thirty-year stalemate, US-Iran negotiations are an encouraging sign of diplomatic-not-military solutions. The Affordable Care Act gives us hope that someday the United States will have Medicare for all. Solar and wind-generated power is growing everywhere, which is very encouraging.

Even as Nelson Mandela grew much older, his mystique and charisma touched the whole world. That he was released after over two decades of imprisonment and didn't harbor any bitterness or hatred but had a positive vision for his country still inspires people everywhere. Knowing of his wisdom and seeing his smiling face both warm our hearts. Here is a person who cared.

We are all inspired by people we know, among our family members and friends, who are daily caring for their children, their spouses, their parents, their coworkers, and their work with integrity and love. Let's continue to inspire each other with our efforts to create a better world, community by community, organization by organization.

OK, who or what inspires you?

————

Aruba—An Enlightened Society?

The following is a reflection on a country as a global leader and a university as a societal leader.

Bhutan has declared to the world that it is creating a society of national happiness. Author Jeremy Rifkin has written about the coming of an empathic civilization. I have written a blog dedicated to the emergence of a compassionate civilization. Recently, I have become aware that the new rector (head) of the University of Aruba has challenged his country to become an enlightened society.

Beautiful Aruba is a country of just over one hundred thousand people that is just seventeen miles long and six miles wide. It is a tourist mecca with gorgeous beaches and a rich diversity of cultures and languages, along with much suffering.

A few years ago, the rector of the university said the following in his inaugural speech:

Aruba could become an enlightened society. An enlightened society is a community continuously developing its consciousness and in which the pursuit of happiness through peace and the rule of justice are the aim of all…Aruba needs to deepen its self-consciousness, its sense of being, belonging, and contributing to an elevated existence of humanity. For this, we need to study ourselves, find ways to better ourselves, and then reach out to the world to help humanity in its further development…What if we research, discover, develop, and find a way to deploy the [unique] qualities we exhibit? I am convinced that the university can help to do this.

What would it look like to awaken a whole country—to make understanding, peace, happiness, and compassion the purpose of being a global-local citizen? How could this be done? How could a university be the catalyst for this noble endeavor?

How might Aruba show the world how to deal with challenges of climate chaos, gender inequality, socioeconomic injustice, elitist governance, and cultural intolerance?

On a recent teaching mission at the University of Aruba, I met this remarkable rector and other educators and citizens of Aruba, and I experienced that this vision is indeed possible to be realized. May it be so.

———

Elder as Prophet

My dad used to say, "Son, don't get old, it isn't any fun." And I would say, "But, Dad, what's the alternative—to die young?" If we are given the gift of old age, what can we do with it? I believe that the elder can be a prophet calling people to prepare for what is coming.

Whether or not we had a career or a family, as we move into our elder years, we can be a voice of truth bringing a sense of urgency into the present. We don't have to worry about what others think of us. We can live utterly on behalf of the coming generations of life on Earth.

We can call people to pay attention to the juggernauts of history rolling down on us. Prepare ye the way for climate chaos! It's coming, for sure. Stop using fossil fuels now. Move away from bodies of water. Get a storm shelter. Grow your own food. Live near your extended family and friends for mutual support.

The elder as prophet can take risks a person with family and work responsibilities cannot so easily take. The elder can participate in nonviolent demonstrations. The elder can write frank Op-Eds to the local paper and sign every relevant petition. The elder can speak out at community meetings. The elder can donate to important causes. The elder can speak at schools to awaken the young. The elder can help get out the vote and volunteer at the voting site.

The elder can maintain a healthy body and mind so that he or she can continue to serve others. The elder can volunteer at the local food bank or soup kitchen. The elder can give courage to younger people. The elder can show others how to be a human being who is aging self-consciously in gratitude for life itself. The elder can learn and do something new every day.

The elder can be "fierce with age" without apology. The elder can be gracious and yet firm, patient and yet impatient. The elder can invite people to wake up and live life with authenticity and passion. The elder can be active on social media, bringing critical news to the attention of others. The elder can honor death and celebrate the passing of friends, foes, and the homeless.

The elder can show others how to die with dignity and trust. The elder can show others how to live with love and laughter. The elder can show others how to be honest and inquisitive about sickness and old age. The elder can be a wonderful grandparent and great-grandparent. The elder can be a sacred sign of living life fully to the last breath. The elder can call people to dream about the coming civilization of compassion and to work for its realization. Yes!

———

Systems Change from Within
The following is a reflection on systemic leadership.

We are all part of the systems in which we find ourselves. This includes economic, political, cultural, and environmental systems. Try as we may, we cannot extricate ourselves from them. We are embedded in historical time and place. This is both bad news and good news. The bad news is that no one has clean hands. The good news is that a system can be perturbed from anywhere within it, thus provoking systems change. Since we are part of a system, we can change it from within.

Rosa Parks perturbed the justice system from inside a bus. Elizabeth Warren is perturbing the financial system from inside the Senate. Because we are citizens, our votes can perturb the governance system. Because we are consumers, our purchases can perturb the economic system. Our friendships can perturb the cultural system. Our ideas can perturb systems of assumptions and common sense.

We find ourselves in an unjust, unequal, unsustainable, plutocratic, intolerant, and violent societal system. From within this system, our every word and deed based in justice, equality, sustainability, participation, tolerance, and nonviolence sends ripples throughout the system, disturbing its equilibrium. When a critical threshold is reached, the very nature and structure of the system is transformed.

Witness the challenge to the divine right of kings and the rise of democracies. Witness the legal changes supporting sexual and racial equality. Witness the fall of the Berlin Wall and monolithic communism. Witness the collapse of apartheid in South Africa. Witness the ban on smoking. Witness the changes in views on marriage rights. And on and on...

Fortunately, there is only change. Nothing stays the same. The question is, where do we need to be headed next? What change can be around the corner if we each nudge in that direction?

———

CHAPTER 6

GLOBAL-LOCAL CITIZENSHIP

W hat is a global-local citizen? How are those who would catalyze a compassionate civilization global-local citizens?

We are all earthlings, evolving from Earth, part of Earth, and stewards of Earth. "I am a citizen of the world," wrote Diogenes Laertius, Greek philosopher (AD 220). Thomas Paine, American revolutionary (AD 1776), wrote, "The world is my country, all [humankind] are my [sisters and brothers], and to do good is my religion." I was born in a small town in Oklahoma, went around Earth at twenty-four, and fell in love with Earth and her earthlings. Who has traveled to other countries? Who has lived in other countries? Who was born in another country? But I say to you, anyone in any circumstance can be a global-local citizen.

The Universe Story

An Exquisitely Special Story

Somewhere in the unimaginable vastness of the cosmos lives a beautiful spiral galaxy. Even with billions of galaxies, there is one that some say is exquisitely special. Some know her as "Milky Way." The wide embracing arms of the galaxy sweep majestically in the same direction around the blinding black hole at its center. Even while rotating like a colossal pinwheel, the galaxy as a whole moves through vast space.

Among billions of stars in the galaxy, in the outskirts of one of its sweeping arms, there lives a star that some say is exquisitely special. Some know him as "Sun."

As this star circles around the galaxy along with its brother stars in its spiral arm, and as the galaxy itself moves through vast space, a family of planets encircles this star. Each in its own orbit, the planets swing around the star, all in the same direction, although on different planes and at different distances from the blazing source of light and heat at their common center. Some say that one of these planets is exquisitely special. Some call her "Earth" or "Gaia."

As this planet itself rotates on an imaginary axis, encircling its star, which swings around the galaxy, which moves through vast space, after two billion years there emerge from the dance of light, water, gravity, air, and heat exquisitely special phenomena. Some call these phenomena "living beings."

After another two billion years (and only two hundred thousand years from today), and after the emergence, transformation, and passing away of unimaginable numbers of living beings, there appeared an exquisitely special creature. Some call them "human beings" or "people."

These creatures woke up, stood up, looked around, and named everything they saw or could think of. They named themselves "human beings," and they named other creatures "living beings," "Earth," "Sun," "Milky Way," and "cosmos." And in so doing, the human beings shook with awe and experienced fear and fascination with all things that were indeed exquisitely special. And they named the mysterious power that is in the midst of and behind all things and that brings all things into being and takes all things out of being— "God," "Goddess," "Great Spirit," "Allah," "Buddha-nature," "Son of God," "Holy Spirit," "Shiva," and many other wonderful names.

And thus, the exquisitely special work of these humans is to cherish every other human and every other creature, whether big or small, whether near or far; every planet, star, and galaxy; and the vast cosmos itself as holy and filled with awe and light and warmth and worthy of being exquisitely special.

The End

The Beginning

"Earth Had a Dream"

Earth had a dream called history
but a flicker, fluttering frames of light—
a few seconds (twelve thousand years?)
after four billion years of slumber,
a wakeful dream, a dream about
"hominization"—
or was it her-story?

DNA, radiation belts, the I Ching,
a unified resonant field theory,
off and on, binary crossover,
flung from unity-consciousness
into the field of yin and yang,
male and female, God and human,
good and bad, plus and minus,
darkness and light,
blinking, twinkling on and off,
the language of space-time,
history-consciousness—
sprung from cosmic radiation
and shifting tectonics,
and the pulses of civilization,
emergent human
between heaven and Earth,
geomancy and holonomics,
the noosphere spun out,
double-helix spinning,

and now
we enter
The Solar Age
Our Star
Energy
for a few more billion years

waking from amnesia
from a pseudo-one-dimensionality
toward the One-without-a-second,
through two-of-a-kind
for now

Psi-bank unfolding, the unconscious,
the archetypes,
vibrational frequencies,
we are all contemporaries,
Gilgamesh and Buddha,
Sister Teresa and Eve,
Moses and Jesus,
Mother Teresa and Hildegard,
Mohammed and Gandhi,
Athena and Margaret,
the computer-of-the-year,
Earth unfolding
her majestic communion of
bacteria,
attunement with the
eternal present,
from her perspective (and his)

the baby cries
the god-man dies

Quetzalcoatl doth arise
and the Virgin smiles
in compassionate radiance

forever

———

What Is A Human Being Anyway?

Fragments of a New Social Philosophy

I believe that if we are to survive as a species, we must reflect on and redefine what a human being is and what a society is for the sake of the future evolution of life on Earth.

What is a human being?

A human being is consciousness of consciousness of consciousness. Or said another way, a human being is a hyper-self-conscious living earthling. But this is not all. Human beings are communal/social beings. We are not born as human beings. We are gradually formed into being human beings through an extensive, subtle process of socialization beginning at birth and continuing throughout a lifetime. We are given language, culture, history, identity, and worldview by a family of origin, a community, a nation, and a planetary ecology of humanness. We then each gradually fashion our own unique variation of self-identity, worldview, and expression from what we have been given, our natural propensities, our experience, our learning, and our imagination.

A human being is one of many self-conscious life-forms of planet Earth, a mammalian animal among other animals and plant life. In our time, the human species has achieved a magnitude of dominance on our planet that is endangering other life-forms and the very ecosystems of Earth. We must change rapidly if we are to survive. We have done this many times before over these two million years of hominid development, two hundred thousand years of *Homo sapiens* development, fifty thousand years of *Homo sapiens*

sapiens development, and five thousand years of historical civilizational development.

Some human beings' consciousnesses are based primarily on contemporary interpretations of ancient myths from religion and culture. Other humans live out of scientific interpretations of empirical data. Still others live out of popular meaning structures provided to them through advertising, television, movies, video games, and the Internet.

We are not only hyperconscious and communal. At its foundation, our consciousness is empathic. The mirror neurons in the brain make us feel what we see others feel. But there is more. We foundationally want to be with others, be helpful to them, care for them, love them, and be acknowledged and loved by them. This is our true nature.

What is human society?

Human society is not simply a collection of isolated individual human beings but rather a single, organic, integrated living system that itself is an organic, integrated part of planet Earth. Without human society, there are no individual human beings. Without Earth, there is no human society. Therefore, as individual human beings, we have an unparalleled debt to and responsibility for both society and Earth.

We are all interdependent and arising in co-origination. My well-being as an individual human being is dependent on the well-being of human society and Earth. I am called to respond in gratitude to and care for these two nested systems of my life and of all our lives. Not only did I not build it, I was built by and for them.

If I am in disrelationship to human society and to Earth, I have lost my way, my true nature, my heart, and my reason for being. When my paltry ego and skin bag have become more important to me than the well-being of my fellow and sister human beings and Earth's community, then I have turned my back on being a human being.

May we awaken moment by moment to being the servant and lover of human society Earth.

———

Big Bang to Human Being

One of the courses I teach at New York University Wagner Graduate School of Public Service is entitled Innovative Leadership for Sustainable Human Development. The first module is on international development and is followed by four modules on leadership, including systems design, group facilitation, cultural evolution, and personal awareness. The course is based on a framework adapted from Ken Wilber's integral quadrants.

Each year, I begin the module on development with an overview of the 13.7 billion years that have brought us to the present moment. I remind my students that we are here now because of an unbroken journey of cause and effect over this mind-boggling time frame—from the big bang to the formation of stars, to planets, to life, to human beings. I then raise two questions: What is a human being? What is development? After discussing this, we review the history of international development over the past one hundred years from economic, to socioeconomic, to sustainable human development, to integral development.

I am convinced that this "story of everything" is the necessary context for our make-or-break moment in human history and evolution. By expanding our sense of time, space, and relations, we gain the needed perspective and knowledge for breakthrough innovations in leadership for development.

For many years, I have been a big fan of *The Universe Story*, written by Thomas Berry and Brian Swimme. This is a beautifully written and scientifically sound narrative of our 13.7-billion-year story, an excerpt of which is required reading for my students. Therefore, you can imagine my recent delight upon learning about the Big History Project. This is an endeavor that seeks to popularize the 13.7-billion-year story of evolution and history as the basis of what it means to be an aware and educated person in the twenty-first century. This story is indeed breathtaking and can fill us with awe and fascination at the preciousness of being human and our unlimited potential for understanding and compassion.

We Are Human Beings First

We are human beings first,
and then we are a sex, a gender, an age, a race,
an ethnicity, a religious conviction, a nationality,
a political persuasion, a sexual orientation,
an economic class, an educational level.

No, actually we aren't a human being first.

First, we are part of this mysterious Cosmos,
then we are part of the Milky Way,
then the solar system,
then the living Earth,
then we are an animal,
a mammal,
then we are hominids,
and THEN we are human beings.

We do have a lot in common with all our
sisters and brothers, yes?
And what is this family resemblance?
Each of us emerged from what had come before
We each change continually
We are interdependent in co-origination
We are empty of a separate self
We each grow old and pass away
And thus we shout out:
Solidarity!
Love!
Mystery!

———

An Example

The Global Citizen: A Love Story

The following was first published in 2007 in Life Lessons for Loving the Way You Live *by Jack Canfield, Mark Victor Hansen, and Jennifer Read Hawthorne. It is included here for your reflection on one example of being a global-local citizen.*

I grew up in a small Oklahoma town. I was raised in a happy, religious home; had perfect attendance in Sunday school; and was an A student. But I often felt that I didn't fully belong where I was. I was taught to "love my neighbor," but I noticed that the African Americans who worked in our town actually lived outside it in other small towns, to which they returned every day after work.

This subtle awareness of social issues was furthered by a small current events newspaper we got in elementary school. Even at that young age, I was touched to read about the United Nations. I sensed something beautiful and expansive about an organization concerned with the whole Earth and the understanding that everyone should have an adequate life.

By the time I reached college, I strongly disliked social injustice of any kind. I became active in the civil rights and women's rights movements—and even led a protest over a policy prohibiting female students from wearing pants in the library and having a curfew! But my first great awakening occurred when, in my junior year, a group of fellow students and I drove to Chicago for a weekend seminar on the "Theological Revolution of the 20th Century," conducted by the Ecumenical Institute.

The seminar was held in an African American ghetto, where the Ecumenical Institute was trying to create a model of renewed community. The contrasts were great: I was used to neat Oklahoma towns and a well-kept college campus; here, I was surrounded by broken glass, burned-out cars, and garbage everywhere.

But something even more astonishing was happening inside at the seminar. We were dialoguing with some of the greatest theologians of our time, discussing age-old questions about divinity, the reality of life, and the search for meaning. By the end of the weekend, I was experiencing the truth of Paul Tillich's teaching, that each of us is fully "accepted" just as we are. We don't have to seek another life, another situation, or another condition; our life is perfect just as it is. Before the weekend, I had always felt shy and alienated; I now felt an interior explosion of healing and goodness and perfection.

And I wanted to share that! After a month-long course at the Ecumenical Institute in the ghetto right after graduating, I realized I had a mission—I was a mission. I could give my life to helping create a different kind of world, where everyone could realize his or her potential. I attended theological seminary and decided to intern with the institute. I fell in love with a wonderful woman, and we soon married. But I would also soon fall in love with and marry a beautiful planet. It was to be my second great awakening.

By this time, the Ecumenical Institute had evolved into its secular form, the Institute of Cultural Affairs. This institute was all about helping people realize what was possible and creating a new world of justice, peace, and hope. A group of institute colleagues decided to take a trip around the world, not as tourists but as people who wanted to know how we could open ourselves to the raw experience of the world—to its beauty, its suffering, its reality, its diversity. We wanted passionately to be in intimate dialogue with it all.

Our plan was ambitious: around the world in thirty-two days. By changing cultures every two or three days—customs, climate, terrain, food, language—we knew we would create a sensory, psychological, mythic, and spiritual overload. And that's what we wanted: not just to observe the world, but also to be the world—the world we wanted to serve.

As we touched down around the globe, I was filled with awe by our planet's vast oceans, jagged peaks, sprawling cities, wildly diverse cultures, and masses of beautiful people. I experienced the powerful mystery of the Aztecs, the sublime beauty of a Shinto shrine, the vitality of Hong Kong, the sultry weather of Manila, the serenity of the Emerald Buddha, a live-goat sacrifice in a Hindu temple, a visit with the China-Lama in Kathmandu, the site where Buddha had his enlightenment and gave his first sermon, the devastating poverty of Calcutta, the birthday celebration of Emperor Haile Selassie in Addis Ababa, the decaying grandeur of Greek and Roman civilization, the awesome beauty of the Vatican, the wonders of a medieval walled city in Dubrovnik, a coming-home experience in the British Isles, and the eternal day of Iceland.

Our accommodations were simple: a church basement, a small hotel. Conditions were uncomfortable, even unbearable at times. My little hotel room in New Delhi felt like a blast furnace from the hot wind blowing through. Sometimes, we were sick. I became dizzy and almost fainted when I saw that goat killed in Nepal. But we wanted to experience what other people experience.

At the end of the adventure, we stopped in Iceland, where all twenty-five of us shared our thoughts about everything we had encountered, trying to "squeeze the meaning" out of our experience. We had become global citizens. We had discovered that while cultures may be different, people are the same. Everyone wants enough food and shelter. They want to be happy, and they want their children to be happy. They have different symbols. They might eat with chopsticks or a fork. They might have a statue or an image or no image. But the human striving is first to survive and then go beyond survival to beauty and truth and union with the divine.

After that trip, I was never, ever the same. I was in love with Mother Earth and with humanity at large. I had been touched by tragic suffering, sublime beauty, spiritual genius, and the ecstasy of being human on this magnificent planet. I had come home. Mother Earth had hugged me—and I had to respond. I had to give my life, my love, my action—to make a difference, to relieve suffering, to advance the human condition. Nothing else would be enough. As a child of Earth, a child of Humanity, I knew it was my duty to serve my people and my planet.

Before this time, I had never left my own nation. After this time, I would spend thirty-five years living in, working in, and visiting fifty-five countries around the world.

For the next twenty years, with my wife and two young sons, I lived and worked in urban slums and poor rural villages in Malaysia, the Republic of Korea, the United States, Jamaica, and Venezuela. We were not well-paid consultants driving in to give advice to the poor. In a Korean village, we lived in a rock-and-mud thatched-roof house. In Jamaica, our sons attended a one-room schoolhouse with three hundred students in a mountain village. I was passionately committed to changing human history, to helping reinvent societies that worked for everyone.

But my childhood reveries came true when I was asked to work for the United Nations. My UN passport was a tangible, magical symbol of my global citizenship. I was being called to transpose my experience from the grassroots-project level to the global-policy level.

I have helped local people around the world improve sanitation, waste management, recycling, water supplies, air quality, environmental health, education, and income. I have helped them prevent the depletion of shellfish stocks in Brazil, plant trees in Egypt, and dig drainage ditches in Tanzania. I have been overwhelmed with the vitality, hope, and hard work of local people regardless of nation, culture, or religion; whether rural or urban; women or men. The heroes were always the local people. I was only a catalyst, a choreographer of change, a social artist.

This small-town Oklahoma boy has lived his life in love with the world. And what a beautiful world it is—full of suffering and happiness, squalor and grandeur. I have received infinitely more gifts from my beloved Earth than I have given her. She is much more gracious and generous, lavishing joy and sorrow, understanding and mystery with immense and exquisite compassion.

And how does my love story with Earth continue? My wife of thirty-five years passed away, and my sons are grown men. I am ready for the next global-local adventure. In fact, having recently retired from the UN, I am on a one-year sabbatical that includes becoming engaged to a most amazing woman, consulting for the UN, teaching graduate school to international students, caring for my elderly mother, and developing my dancing skills. What will life offer and require of me—and you—next? Whatever it is, we are the people, and now is the time.

———

The Dance of Life

It finally happened. My sixteen years as a UN international civil servant and policy advisor came to a close due to mandatory age-related retirement at sixty-two. I have loved being with the UN for these years just as I loved being with the Institute of Cultural Affairs (ICA) for the previous twenty-one years. Now a new chapter opens, a new dance begins. What is that dance?

Over the past three years, I have written many times in my journal about this new dance. It includes a life of meditation, making music, dancing, writing, studying, consulting, teaching, leading retreats, and spending more time with family and friends. Now that the new dance is in motion, it seems chaotic, overwhelming, too much. I have requests to work in Afghanistan, Bangladesh, five African countries, Trinidad, Canada, Garrison, and New York City. How to focus? How to prioritize? How to relax and enjoy each day, each breath? These are the same questions of the previous two chapters. It is all one life, one gesture, one word, one deed, and then...

To mark this transition, a great celebration was held—the Dance of Life. Sixty family members and friends from the UN, ICA, Mystery School, Hermitage Heart, and the Garrison community joined the dance, representing fifteen countries. Another sixty friends and family sent best wishes. We gathered at my home, "Hillside Cottage" in the Hudson Valley, on a bright summer day. We celebrated many great turnings of life's dance: birth (my mother's eighty-sixth and my sixty-second), adoption (my son Benjamin's), marriage (my son Christopher and Jennifer's first wedding anniversary), retirement (mine), and death (the third anniversary of my wife Mary's passing). All these events had July dates. In addition, we celebrated my new relationship with a truly great being.

What a great celebration it was! We danced Enos Mythos, an ancient Greek circle dance of deep recognition. A UN colleague played the violin beautifully. My sister-in-law performed an interpretive dance accompanied by my brother and nephew. A neighbor played the harp. I danced while a special guest singer sang, "I Hope You Dance." A friend from California read a poem. An ICA colleague of thirty years sang a love song. Another longtime colleague facilitated much of the event. My brother thanked me for teaching him the letter *e*. My dance teacher evoked generous gestures from the group. My niece prepared a three-layer buttercream cake. People spoke many kind words. Guests brought ethnic dishes to diversify the buffet. We ate delicious food and drank sparkling cider. It was truly a magical moment for everyone. What a blessing to live life fully and to celebrate it with family and friends.

And now what? The future beckons, blowing wildly in my face. My soul longs for rest, reflection, expression, and integration. The suffering world waits expectantly. I pray for strength and courage. I vow to dance on in passionate compassion.

There is only the dance!

———

The UN and the Jacaranda Tree

Nairobi is happily filled with these beautiful blue trees this time of year, but only for about a month. Then, we must wait another eleven. Seasons are punctuated by the short rain and the long rain. But of course with climate chaos, things are changing. The skies now are so clear and bright with flowers of gold, red, and white everywhere.

The Westgate massacre is still fresh in people's minds, creating increased awareness of their movements, their whereabouts, and what is going on around them. But life goes on. Children go to school. People shop, drive to work, return home, and ride their bicycles in the magnificent forest—said to be the largest inside any city in the world—near the UN compound.

I am only a short ride from the UN and am grateful for the opportunity to be of service to the organization as a consultant after years as a staff member. It continues its "mission impossible" of caring for the whole world with a handful of people and a pocketful of funds. With all its shortcoming and challenges, if we didn't have the UN, we would need to invent it very quickly. Few other institutions bring together every nationality, race, culture, and religion to dialogue and work for peace and development, day after day, in every country on Earth.

UN staff work under great stress in dangerous situations and inside a complex bureaucracy with too much to do and too few resources. Some people are posted without their families. Nevertheless, people come together to make the impossible possible.

May these international civil servants be safe and happy as they serve the least, the lost, and the last and protect Earth herself.

Love of Grandchildren, Mystery of Life

My two grandchildren live twelve hours from me by car or an hour and a half by air. This is far too far. I ache for them, especially after Skype sessions. Even though I spend part of each winter and summer living in their town, it is not enough.

There is some deep connection and affection that I don't fully understand. Of course you can blame it on progeny and the evolutionary drive to procreate. They are carrying my genes into the future after I am gone. But it is not just genes. If my adopted son were to have a child, I would feel just the same. It is much more intimate than that. It is as if I get to grow up again with them.

My grandson Phoenix is five years and nine months old, and my granddaughter Mariela is three years and five months. When I am with them, we sit on the floor and play with Lego bricks, or I read to them. Phoenix has just learned to read. When I go this winter, he will read to me for the first time. He loves his tap dance lessons and is a yellow belt in Ninja Kids Club. He says kindergarten is "awesome!" Mariela enjoys her ballet lessons and going with her mommy to the gym. Needless to say, they are very smart and very good looking (they really are)!

I send them photos, postcards, and gifts from places where I am working, such as New York, Tanzania, Bahrain, and Kenya. But what is it about them that is so fetching? I know that there are billions of children around the world who deserve my allegiance. What is the draw of these two? They are my baby's babies. That is such a profound mystery, the flow onward in time from generation to generation.

I look into the past and see ancestors stretching back over hundreds, thousands, millions of years, even back to the big bang. I look into the future and see descendants stretching forward in time for hundreds, thousands, millions of years. Or will it be so? Will something stop this flow—climate chaos, nuclear holocaust, disease, an asteroid striking Earth? Will our species die out or evolve into another life-form or cyberconscious being? Will other species become dominant—dolphins, whales, elephants, or chimpanzees with their big brains, language, community structures, empathy, and personalities? Or will bacteria be the whole story?

It helps me when I remember that everything that is born dies—every individual and every collective, every animal and every empire. Even Earth herself will become inhospitable to life someday. But will it be in one hundred years or in two billion years? Now, that depends on what we humans do, doesn't it?

Phoenix and Mariela, I love you and all children past, present, and future. What do I need to do today to make that love real, so that you will have a future of compassion and wisdom that is sustainable and just? How can I help you discover who you are and contribute your unique gifts to the civilizing process? I know that is yours alone to do, but your grandpa wants only happiness and peace for you now and always.

———

Korean Vignettes

- I am writing from Seoul, Korea, where I have been for one week. I am filled with many emotions and am making many connections of present-past-future. I am here to facilitate and speak in the UN Public Service Global Forum on Sustainable Development with over one thousand delegates from around the world. One of them is a new colleague from the University of Aruba, whom I met in March when I was teaching in her innovative program on collaborative leadership.

- On this visit, I have been able to see dear friends and colleagues from the time my family lived here from 1972 to 1978. At that time, I was with an NGO, the Institute of Cultural Affairs, doing comprehensive community development in poor villages on Jeju Island and near the demilitarized zone. Our purpose was to help create models for other communities to emulate and was related to the Korean government's Saemaul Undong (New Community Movement). This week, I visited the village near the demilitarized zone, Kuh Du I Ri (Sleeping Dragon Village Two). Well, the sleeping dragon awoke, and the village has transformed into a highly prosperous community. My family of four lived in one room in the back of a store in the village's community center. Those were great days!

- I returned to Korea as a UNDP policy advisor in 1994 and again in 2005. Each time, I was shocked by the rapid developments of Korean society economically, politically, and culturally.

- Yesterday was the sixty-fourth anniversary of the beginning of the Korean War. After that devastating war, Korea was one of the world's poorest countries. Today, South Korea is a major world economic power, the secretary general of the UN is Korean, and people around the world are dancing Gangnam style!

- *In 1917, my great-uncle, after whom both my father and I are named, was a medical missionary in Korea—one of my many mysterious connections with Korea. And of special importance, both of my sons were born here, and one is Korean. What a gift to be related to this beautiful people and land.

- I just had dinner with another wise Korean colleague, who said that the emerging global civilization is about one thing: love. How to realize and embody that in the midst of so much confusion and suffering?

- Korea is now providing financial and technical assistance to poor countries around the world through its international development agency, KOICA. The Korean heart is wide and deep. Koreans have a lot of empathy and concern for those in need. This is my heartfelt experience, not a theory.

The Order Is Dead: Long Live the Order

"The Order is dead." I first heard those words in Mexico in 1988. That was twenty-seven years ago, when the global Panchayat took the global Order Ecumenical, the staff association of the ICA, out of being. No longer would we live by vows of poverty, chastity, and obedience within the structures, assignments, and leadership of our order. It was time to be part of the global movement of those who care.

Since then, former order members have done amazing things with our lives. We have facilitated thousands of events, written hundreds of books, and created the International Association of Facilitators (IAF), as well as many other organizations. We have been educators, consultants, pastors, civil servants, librarians, youth workers, NGO officials (including the ICA), doctors, nurses, business managers, lawyers, artists, spouses, parents, grandparents, and much more.

We have practiced community, organizational, and leadership development. We have spoken out for justice, equality, sustainability, tolerance, and participation. We have served the least, the last, and the lost both nearby and far-flung around this planet. We have grown older, and some of us have died. In fact, many of us have passed on. And eventually, all of us will pass on. What is our legacy? Who are our descendants? Who will carry forward our spirit, vision, mission, methods, and passion?

The young, of course. There will always be those who care in every generation. They are among us even now. They will awaken, equip themselves, and move out in service. They are the sensitive and responsive ones who are ever vigilant and at work in every country and every clime. It is these young ones who will mitigate climate chaos and promote participatory governance, cultural tolerance, socioeconomic justice, and gender equality.

These are our children and grandchildren, the unstoppable movement of those who care. We can count on these young ones. And before we go, we must do everything we can to support, train, and inspire them, our colleagues.

As for me, I am teaching grad students dedicated to public service in how to catalyze societal transformation; how to facilitate;

how to lead; how to carry out strategic management; and how to do international development, human development, and sustainable development of individual mind-sets and behaviors, communities, organizations, cultures, institutions, and systems around the world. And I am a doting grandpa to two remarkable grandchildren.

I am so proud of and hopeful for these young ones. May they carry on, enlarge, deepen, and make more wise and effective anything I have tried to do and invent things I cannot even imagine.

Onward!

———

CHAPTER 7

PRACTICING CARE OF SELF AND OTHERS AS MINDFUL ACTIVISTS

How do we sustain our motivation and energy as innovative leaders and global-local citizens who are part of the movement of movements that is catalyzing a compassionate civilization? What follows are a few reflections on cultivating understanding and compassion; realizing happiness; celebrating gratitude; living lifelong commitment; choosing courage; dancing with time; and embracing sadness, sickness, old age, and death.

Cultivating Understanding and Compassion

Practicing Compassion and Wisdom

It has been said that compassion and wisdom are the two inseparable wings of the bird of awakening, allowing movement through life's often-volatile currents. Compassion is "suffering with" and vowing to relieve another's suffering as one's own. Wisdom is the understanding of the fundamental nature of reality, its utter interdependence, and continuous transformation.

As we negotiate the early years of this make-or-break century, we need to cultivate and manifest these two skillful means in mind, body, heart, speech, and action. Fortunately, there are many practices to help us do this, including meditation, ethical studies, yoga, journaling, movement, art, reading, spending time in nature, volunteering, prayer, contemplation, liturgy, and being part of a practice community. The most important practice, however, is to bring mindfulness and kindness into our daily lives, moment by moment.

Please enjoy the beautiful faces and earnest voices of those you meet who are speaking profound words of compassion and wisdom, of love and truth.

———————

John's Profound Question

"What is the source of compassion?"

A colleague recently posed this question to me. Let's explore his provocative question together. How does compassion manifest itself, and from where does it arise? It seems to me that its basis is a gift of our mammalian heritage.

All mammals have awareness of and empathy with others of their kind. This is true especially of our close relative, the chimpanzee, but it is also true of elephants and dolphins. Neurologically, we know that the mammalian brain's mirror neurons allow one organism to literally experience what it sees happening to another. We warm-blooded mammals have evolved to care about each other and to express affection for each other.

With human beings, this capacity is both deepened and broadened. We feel each other's suffering and desire to help another relieve her or his suffering. We know what our own suffering is like, and we want to relieve it. In like manner, we want to help others relieve their suffering because we know what it is like when it is our own.

But with us, our compassion extends far beyond our own species. We also experience compassion for other animal species and for Earth's plants, water, air, soil, and minerals. This I believe is because we are essentially earthlings and children of the evolving cosmos. Someone has said that we are a star's way of looking at a star. I would add that we are a star's way of loving a star.

Compassion arises from our basic nature of empathy, care, and love—our basic goodness. This is one reason why we are shocked when someone harms another person. It is not expected; it is shocking and is not our usual way of being. We are communal beings. We love to be with others of our kind and to care for each other. The source of compassion is neither more nor less than our very being. Compassion, then, is ontological, as well as biological and sociological. We are the heart, eyes, and hands of compassion itself.

But why then, you ask, do you and I harm others if our basic nature is compassion? Why are there violence, warfare, poverty, and injustice in human society? One answer is that our basic goodness becomes obscured and distorted by negative emotions of fear, anger, hatred, greed, ignorance, jealousy, and pride. Our attachment to what we mistakenly see as our separate self or ego poisons our mind and heart and creates confusion and harmful behavior.

This is why we must continually *practice* letting go of self-attachment and *practice* cherishing others. We must wake up again and again from the nightmare of our confused mind to our true nature of inter-dependence. We must train our minds to follow our deepest impulses—that is, compassion—and not be overtaken by negative emotions.

––––––––

An Epistemology of Compassion

How do we know? How do we know that we know? How do we know what we know? What is required to convince us that we know? Is a statistic, experience, feeling, theory, reference, authority, measurement, experiment, or image that convinces us that we know something?

Take compassion. How do we know compassion? We can read about it. We can ask others about it. We can experience receiving it. We can experience giving it to others. But what is it, and how do we know that it is it?

Compassion is to be with suffering, either someone else's or one's own, and to help relieve that suffering. There are of course many forms of suffering, including pain, anxiety, worry, fear, angst, disorientation, boredom, ignorance, sickness, abuse, dissatisfaction, anguish, loss, grief, humiliation, and on and on. What is involved in being with and relieving our own suffering?

Sometimes, we can relieve our suffering by doing something tangible. If we are hungry, we can eat. But what if there is no food available? If we have a headache, we can take a pain killer. But what if it doesn't help? What if there is nothing tangible to be done to relieve our suffering? Then, we can work with our suffering in the following ways.

First, we can *acknowledge* our particular form or experience of suffering. Then, we can *accept* this particular suffering. Next, we can be utterly *present* to it. We can *comfort* it and be *kind* to our suffering. We can then *recognize* its true nature of impermanence and interdependence—that is, it will not be forever. It will change when causes and conditions change. It will dissipate and become something else. Finally, we can *let go* of our suffering.

Once we have learned how to relieve our own suffering, we can help others relieve theirs. If someone is hungry, we can give him food. If someone is sick, we can take her to a doctor. At the societal level, we can relieve suffering by creating compassionate policies and programs, such as food stamps, universal health care, affordable housing, job training, a living wage, affirmative action, and environmental protection.

If other people's suffering cannot be eradicated by something tangible, however, we can help them alleviate their own suffering using the process we used with ourselves. We can help them acknowledge and accept their own suffering. We can help them be with and comfort their suffering. We can help them recognize that it is not forever and let go of grasping and being grasped by their suffering. We can help them liberate themselves from their suffering and experience gratitude and happiness inherent in being alive.

The epistemology of compassion involves shining the light of awareness on the experience of suffering and letting that pure awareness begin to transform that experience and our relationship to it. May our compassion release and guide us to be there for others, as well as for us.

Daily Vows of Compassion and Wisdom

Fortunately, there are many wonderful religious and spiritual traditions that can help human beings live lives of love and truth. Every morning, I bring my palms together, bow, and make the following vows, taken mostly from traditional Buddhist sources. May this inspire you as it does me.

"I take refuge in the Buddha, the dharma, and the sangha until I realize enlightenment and bring all sentient beings to nirvana."

(Interpretation: I find solace in the inherent capacity to wake up to a life of compassion and understanding, the teachings of compassion and understanding, and the community of those who are continually waking up to compassion and wisdom, until I realize compassion and understanding and help relieve the suffering of every conscious being.)

"Sentient beings are numberless. I vow to save them."

(Interpretation: There are vast numbers of conscious beings. I vow to relieve their suffering and help them realize compassion and understanding.)

"Desires are inexhaustible. I vow to put an end to them."

(Interpretation: Desires arise continually making their demands on us. I vow to place a limit to them and their influence.)

"The dharmas are boundless. I vow to master them."

(Interpretation: There are vast numbers of phenomena. I vow to understand and work skillfully with them all.)

"The Buddha Way is unattainable. I vow to attain it."

(Interpretation: The pathway of waking up to compassion and understanding continues to unfold. I vow to realize it moment by moment.)

"May all sentient beings realize peace, happiness, wisdom, and compassion."

(Interpretation: May all conscious beings realize the peace found in acceptance, the happiness found in gratitude and making others happy, the wisdom of understanding relative and absolute truth, and the compassion of relieving the suffering of all beings.)

"May all beings in the six worlds realize peace, happiness, wisdom, and compassion."

(Interpretation: May everyone who has died and also those still living realize the peace found in acceptance, the happiness found in gratitude and making others happy, the wisdom of understanding relative and absolute truth, and the compassion of relieving the suffering of all beings.)

"I take the backward step to study the Buddha Way, which is to study the self, which is to forget the self, which is to be awakened by the ten thousand things, which is to drop off body and mind, which is to let go, which is to let go of letting go."

(Interpretation: I turn inward to contemplate and study how to continually wake up and live a life of compassion and understanding, which is to study the nature of the self; which is to realize that there is no separate, permanent self; which is awakened by everything we encounter; which is to dis-identify with my particular body and mind; which is to live in detached engagement; which is to live in detached engagement about living in detached engagement.)

"Earth, fire, water, air, all dharmas manifest emptiness, impermanence, and suffering, thus realizing that all is good, the self is accepted, the past is approved, and the future is open."

(Interpretation: All phenomena have the characteristics of interdependence and continual change and anxiety concerning these characteristics, and it is in the midst of this awareness we can realize that everything that we are given in life is perfect; that this interdependent, ever-changing, anxious self is perfect; that everything that has ever happened has brought us to this perfect moment; and that the future is to be decided and created by those who live their lives.)

"*Om mani padme hum.*"

(Translation: Hail, Jewel in the Lotus! Interpretation: I heartily acknowledge those who embody perfect compassion and understanding!)

"*Gate gate, paragate, parasamgate odhi svaha.*" (Prajna Heart Sutra)

(Translation: Gone, gone, completely gone, everyone gone to the other shore, enlightenment, hail! Interpretation: May everyone realize perfect compassion and understanding!)

Realizing Happiness

Happiness, Joy, and Pleasure

Happiness is a state of accepting what is, with gratitude and wonder. Joy is when we bubble over with excitement because of something or someone we have encountered. Pleasure is a feeling of sensory delight of taste, touch, smell, sound, or sight.

Happiness is waking up to the realization that we are alive, aware, and in love with life. Joy is a thrill of satisfaction, pride, or affection. Pleasure is a sensation of warmth, comfort, or stimulation.

Happiness is just being, just breathing, just sitting, just walking. Joy is a burst of surprise or elation. Pleasure is an animal sense of being grounded in nature and in physicality.

Happiness is the birthright of sentience. Joy is an unexpected gift. Pleasure is a warm stomach or a tingling in the chest.

Happiness is the experience of making others happy. Joy is a sunrise in the mind. Pleasure is a deep sigh.

Happiness is a way of living, joy is an irrepressible smile, and pleasure is a sip of tea.

May all beings everywhere realize happiness, joy, and pleasure. May we help relieve the suffering and pain of all beings. May the happiness, joy, and pleasure of a compassionate civilization rise up in our heart, our mind, and our body. May a compassionate civilization be manifest in time and space through our words, our deeds, and our lifestyle. May it be really so, even now.

———

How to Be Happy

To be conscious involves living in many different realities simultaneously or in rapid succession. We all experience this. One moment, we are in love with life—the beauty of the sun glinting off the freshly fallen snow. The next moment, we are aware of massive suffering around us—the twenty-two thousand homeless children in New York City. Then, we find ourselves focused on a mundane task, say, washing dishes. Suddenly, our mind is filled with worry about work or health. Later, we are relaxed in a kind of steady state of sufficiency. Then, we find ourselves in conflict with someone we love. And so it goes throughout a day. We all know about the roller coaster of situations and emotions to which we are subject.

There are times when we are overflowing with hope and possibility. At other times, we fall into despair or depression. We have moments of great certitude concerning the perfection and goodness of this life. And there are times when we are full of doubt concerning the meaning of life and death. These are the normal fluctuations of consciousness moving through time and space and responding emotionally, mentally, and physically, moment by moment.

In the midst of these seemingly contradictory states of consciousness, how do we maintain equilibrium, equanimity, and momentum? How do we move from caring for our mundane existence to dreaming big dreams for self, family, and society; to experiencing pain and confusion; to enjoying being alive; to facing our own mortality; or to working to catalyze a new world that works for everyone?

One profound insight concerning relating to these fluctuations of consciousness has to do with learning to tolerate cognitive dissonance of the relative and the absolute. Our relative reality has to do with whatever fleeting situations and emotions we are experiencing from moment to moment. The absolute has to do with the realization that all of it is perfect. In as much as we embrace impermanence, interdependence, and suffering as perfect, we experience happiness and peace.

It is all good. And it is with this understanding that we can relax in gratitude and extend boundless compassion to our fellow and sister beings and to ourselves.

———

The Miracle of Happiness

Tragedy has to do with coming to ruin, extreme sorrow, the disastrous, and the calamitous. Does this not describe human existence exactly? As human beings, we are fraught with anxiety about our survival, our identity, our status, our possessions, and our relationships; we suffer horrible diseases of body and mind; we lose those we dearly love; and then we die, each one of us. Is that not coming to ruin? Is such an existence not filled with sorrow? Is this not the story of disaster and calamity?

So, what can you and I do when we become aware that human life—our life—is tragic? What are our options?

We can despair and curse our existence. Or we can delude ourselves by turning our back on the glaring evidence and fight for as much pleasure, comfort, status, and power as possible. Or we can have compassion for ourselves and everyone we encounter, acknowledging their and our own suffering and vowing to relieve as much of it as possible, bringing into being the miracles of peace and happiness.

I choose the latter. By acknowledging and accepting the universal nature of impermanence, suffering, and interbeing, we can literally transform our relationship to our lives and to our relationships. We can turn tragedy into treasure, sorrow into sustenance, disaster into determination, and calamity into calmness.

Nothing life brings can separate us from the ecstatic gift of being alive for this precious moment. Let's celebrate truth, beauty, and love. Let's champion justice for all. Let's practice kindness and generosity rather than living out of fear, anger, hatred, and greed.

This is our chance. Let's live our lives with abandon and passion. What do we have to lose?

———

Celebrating Gratitude

Gifts, Generosity, and Gratitude

Everything that is, everything we are, and everything we have is a gift. Gratitude, therefore, is the most natural emotion and response we can have as a human being. The universe itself is a mysterious gift, including our nearby star that shares its light and warmth freely, generously. Gratitude is the natural response.

Planet Earth herself is a gift, giving life-giving gifts of water, air, soil, plants, animals, and humans freely, generously. Gratitude is the natural response. The human community, including the family into which we are born, is a gift provided freely, generously. Gratitude is the natural response.

Our body-mind is a gift given freely, generously. Gratitude is the natural response. Our language, culture, and religion are gifts given freely, generously. Gratitude is the natural response. Other people grow crops and provide the food that sustains us. Gratitude to farmers, truckers, and grocery store workers.

Other people build the houses that shelter us. Gratitude to architects, contractors, and construction workers. Other people provide the education that nurtures our minds. Gratitude to curriculum developers, teachers, and administrators.

Other people provide the clothes that protect us. Gratitude to clothing designers, seamstresses, and store workers. And so it goes. We are each enabled to live our lives through the gifts given generously by our fellow and sister human beings. For this, we are grateful.

We each share our gifts with others. The whole human family is sustained through the sharing of gifts. For this, we are grateful. Some people receive more gifts than others. Others give more gifts than others. May we each be overwhelmed by generosity and gratitude.

As for me, I am grateful for gratitude itself.

———

Reflections on a Cold, Windy Afternoon

The wind cuts like a knife. It is too cold to be outside. Living right on the Hudson River means even colder and windier conditions. The sky is a pale blue with a few white clouds. The sun shines brightly, but it is still frigid. I have completed teaching one course and am beginning to think about Thanksgiving and then travelling to Asheville, North Carolina, to spend winter near the grandkids. I still have papers to grade and another course to complete.

My travels to Nairobi have shifted to January. My mind drifts into the near future in Asheville and Nairobi even though I am still here in New York. How bad will the winter be? I've heard predictions of a lot of snow. How much have the grandkids grown? It will be delightful to be with them again. Will Nairobi be safe? It will be great to do some work there for the UN. How will the jet lag be this time? I'm looking forward to returning to Oklahoma, my home state, in March to speak at a peace symposium and then to teaching in Aruba.

In eight months, I turn seventy—the new fifty. But it is still seventy, seven decades on our beautiful planet Earth. What a journey. What a blessing. What is there still to do and be and know? After four and a half decades of doing international development in fifty-five countries, what is now being asked of me? I still have energy and passion. I still want to serve.

I want to continue my teaching and consulting, my writing and speaking—but for how long? Until I am eighty or ninety? Do I have ten years or twenty, or less or more? What would be the greatest contribution I could make? Should I publish my memoir now? Should I write a book on a compassionate civilization? Should I assist 350.org in mitigating climate chaos? Where am I being called to grow and stretch?

At the same time, I want to spend more time with my grandkids, wife, sons, and brother. I want to have more time to read and reflect. I want to get more rest and exercise. I want to eat a healthy diet. I want to be in good shape until I leave this identity. And until then, I want to focus my energies on catalyzing a hoped-for future of sustainable human development. I want to dream about the evolution of conscious, compassionate life over the next one thousand, one million, one billion years.

I am so grateful for having a life, for being a human being, for waking up again and again to the wonder of being alive in this mysterious cosmos. A gift unasked for and undeserved, and it is yours and mine. This is our moment. Let's use it wisely.

The Christ Word: This Is It!

Waiting.
Longing.

When will someone or something come to make it all OK?
When will someone arrive to transform our situ-
ation so that we can truly live, fully live?
Waiting for so long.
Longing for so much.
And what appears is a helpless baby who
grows in wisdom and love and is execut-
ed by the state at the age of thirty-three.

This one who kept the company of prostitutes and tax
collectors; who threw out the money changers; who
said, "Love your enemies"; surely this cannot be the
one for whom we have been waiting and longing.

But if it were, what is the message we hear and know?
"Don't wait any longer.
No one else is coming.
The fullness of time is now.
We can live and love our lives ful-
ly here and now just as they are."
This message is good and great news indeed, that we
can live our given lives, our real situations as a gift, in
humility, in gratitude, in compassion, in ecstasy.

Yes, this is good news beyond anything
we could ever expect or anticipate.
This is it!

All that is, is good and perfect!

You, just as you are, are accepted and sustained in mystery!

The past, just as it is, is received by history!

The future is wildly open for you to cocreate!

Hallelujah!

Hallelujah!

Hallelujah!

———

Living Lifelong Commitment

How to Live on Behalf of All?

The One Sacred Vow

What does it look like to "live on behalf of all"? How can I, moment by moment, get out on the tip of the wedge blade of history between the no-longer and the not-yet and live my life and die my death on behalf of all beings?

I have already lived a long life, for which I am deeply grateful. I have had many successes, many failings, many lessons, much pleasure, great sadness, and deep happiness. I need nothing more. I vow to give the rest of my life to relieve the suffering of all beings everywhere, thus catalyzing a civilization of compassion and sustainable human development.

There are many distractions—comfort, security, fear, entertainment, food, tiredness, rest, sickness, health, ego, desire, confusion, anger, timidity, errands, nitty-gritties, aesthetics, competition, and demands of others. How will I realize my vow? I will commit to six sacred arenas, five sacred actions, and four sacred practices.

The Six Sacred Arenas

I will focus the energies of my mind, heart, and body on (1) mitigating climate chaos, protecting the natural environment, and supporting renewable energy; (2) expanding and strengthening women's rights and awakening gender equality; (3) promoting participatory governance institutions, policies, and leadership; (4) nurturing cultural and religious tolerance and understanding; (5) creating structures of socioeconomic justice, including universal health, education, and well-being for all; and (6) fostering nonviolence, peace, reconciliation, and prison reform.

The Five Sacred Actions

Within the above six arenas I will (1) write and publish; (2) design and carry out my activism; (3) market my speaking engagements that promote sustainable human development; (4) train groups in innovative leadership methods; and (5) facilitate strategic planning events with groups, networks, and movements.

The Four Sacred Practices

To sustain my commitment to the above vow, arenas, and actions and to deal with many distractions, I will (1) engage in daily meditation, contemplation, prayer, liturgy, and reflection-in-action; (2) regularly deepen my understanding of my vow, arenas, actions, and practices through reading, study, workshops, conferences, and retreats; (3) live and work with like-minded and like-hearted people, in harmony with nature and maintaining a healthy, energized body; and (4) engage in acts of kindness toward everyone I encounter.

May it be so!

What is your vow? What are your arenas, actions, and practices?

Burn Out? Never.

After I had been a UNDP staff member for many years, people would sometimes ask me if I had just joined. When I would ask them why they asked me that, they would say it was because I seemed fresh, positive, and uncynical. I would then say that I had been an international civil servant for fifteen years but that I take care of myself. Every day, I do things that maintain my awareness, integrity, hope, and relevance. Taking care of oneself is very important, but it doesn't happen by accident.

If we don't take care of ourselves, we can burn out or become disillusioned, cynical, complacent, self-satisfied, distracted, or despairing. My definition of a cynic is an idealist who has burned out. Most people begin their lives or careers with hope, vision, and energy. Then, they encounter the "real world" of struggle, egos, resistance, conflict, and failure.

In my twenties, I believed that my NGO and I would transform the world within ten years. In my forties, I believed that the UN and I would transform the world in twenty years. In my sixties, I believe that the human race and I will transform the world within one hundred years. But what will the transformation be? Will we create a compassionate civilization of sustainable human development, or will we live in misery on a degraded planet?

How do we maintain our commitment and passion for transformation as we deal with our aging bodies and the stubborn resistance that we encounter in individual psyches and behaviors and in collective assumptions and institutions? How do we do what needs to be done today while we envision what could be realized in some tomorrow? How do I take care of myself so that I keep on keeping on?

One of the things I do every morning is remember who I am and what I am about. I express gratitude for my life and for life itself. I articulate my vows and intentions. I remember those who have gone before me and those I love. I stand before the really real and rededicate myself to a life of compassion and understanding. I find that this is the most important thing I do all day long. It is my action before the action. In that moment, everything is realized, and I am at peace and ready to know, do, and be all that I can for all that can be.

Act without Any Certainty

Concerning the future of life on Earth, I am both very hopeful and deeply concerned. I am hopeful because I believe that we human beings can indeed wake up and create a compassionate civilization. I am concerned because this is in no way guaranteed, and there are many powerful forces opposing such a transformation.

On the side of hope, we have human nature itself, which is fundamentally good, empathic, and caring. We have a trajectory of history that is toward increased democratic governance, human rights, environmental awareness and protection, gender equality, economic and social justice, and cultural tolerance. We have around the world many individuals of goodwill and their organizations and networks that are working tirelessly to make a better world based on values of sustainability, justice, equality, participation, and understanding.

On the side of concern, we have the powerful negative emotions that plague us human beings—fear, anger, hatred, pride, greed, and ignorance. We have vested economic interests that are fighting to protect and promote wealth based on fossil fuels, armaments, and toxic investments. We have people who are consumed by sexism, racism, and homophobia. We have private citizens who have heavily armed themselves. We have people who do not believe in science and are controlled by beliefs of religious fundamentalism.

How will all of this play out over the next ten years, hundred years, thousand years? It is not at all certain. It behooves each of us to do everything in our power to bend the arc of history toward sustainable human development, toward a compassionate civilization. We need to be ready to take radical action to defend the weak and create a better future for all life on Earth.

It is my sincere belief, without any certainty whatsoever, that light will prevail over darkness, good over evil, reason over fear, freedom over slavery, and life over death. In this noble endeavor, our most cherished tools are truth, kindness, understanding, nonviolence, solidarity, vision, strength, and courage. As we continue on the journey, let us do so with open eyes and a joyous heart.

Never Enough, yet Sufficient

Nothing we do is enough. There is always more to do—more people to love, more work to be done.

It seems that I especially do so little, with teaching a course here, conducting a consultancy there, writing e-mails every day, writing a blog now and then, and being with those I love when I can. It is all so little. What can the impact be? I need more time, more energy. I need to be in many places at once. But what could ever be enough?

How many patients can a doctor see in a day? There are always more to be seen. How many people can you really touch with a kind word or a helpful action? It seems it is so few. When we have been given the gift of life, unasked for and undeserved, how can we ever give enough in return?

Yet what we do is somehow sufficient. It is our gift given back, our reaching out to others. It is the way we touch the whole, one at a time. Then, those we have touched touch others, and so on until the whole of humanity and Earth are touched.

We share our speech and our deeds; we invest them in the community. They ripple outward, endlessly. We also receive energy from others who touch us, encourage us, and care for us. It is all we can do, to share and to receive.

How much do I love, both in giving and in receiving? It is never enough. Yet in some mysterious way, it is sufficient, even perfect.

How can I vow daily to save all sentient beings? Is that not utterly impossible? Whether it is reasonable to so intend, it is still my earnest vow and hope. It encourages me to do more, to be more, moment by moment. And it inspires me with a vision of a compassionate civilization that is always coming to be.

———

Choosing Courage

Change, Courage, Serenity, and Wisdom

May I realize "the serenity to accept the things I cannot change, the courage to change the things I can, and the wisdom to know the difference."

This quote by theologian Reinhold Niebuhr was one of my mother's favorites. She wrote it out in elegant script, had it framed, and also made it into note cards. It provided solace to my mother as she lived each day. It appeared in my mind recently as I was analyzing a series of decisions and actions. What does it mean? How could it help me or you?

The operative word in the quote is *wisdom*. How do I discern the difference between what I cannot change and what I can? The other key concepts are serenity, acceptance, courage, change, knowing, and difference.

What are things I cannot change? Death, old age, and illness come to mind, both for those I love and for me. How do I cultivate acceptance and serenity in relation to each of these? We must acknowledge them, understand them, embrace them, and live them with gratitude, letting go of worry and fear. What about things that I think I cannot change but actually are changeable? Should we accept with despair or serenity unjust systems and corrupt institutions that may seem impossible to change? History shows that they can be changed with the unflagging efforts of many people over time. What we each do matters, yet our whole life may be lived within an unjust system.

What are things that I can change? My own and other people's attitudes, behaviors, and relationships can be changed, *but it is not easy*. Cultural values, policies, laws, and institutional arrangements can be changed—also not easy. How do I build up the necessary courage and commitment to change them when they seem so intractable? We can acknowledge, understand, and work with them so that they evolve into something new, from negative and harmful to positive and healthy. What are things that I think that I can change that actually might be unchangeable by me? I usually cannot change other people's attitudes, behaviors, cultures, religions, or institutions. We can dialogue or teach about or model new options for other people, but we cannot force them to change. We must accept them as they are with serenity and love and hope for some future change.

And how do we learn to discern and know the difference between what can or cannot be changed? This takes a lifetime of moment-by-moment attention, analysis, trial, and error. Can it be changed? Try. Did it work or not? Why? Can it not be changed? Try again. What happened this time? Why? It takes both serenity and courage, both acceptance and changing things to develop the wisdom to know the difference.

May we remain open to learning by doing, risking possibility, and accepting limits, from womb to tomb. And may this be our happiness and fulfillment.

———

Should I Go to Nairobi?

The following reflection was written a few years ago when I was weighing up going to Nairobi after a time of violence.

Tonight, I am preparing to teach a graduate class tomorrow and to leave Friday for Nairobi on a UN assignment. I was wondering if I had time to blog. I am not ready yet to brainstorm strategies that will deal with what is blocking the realization of a compassionate civilization. So, I thought that I could discuss how we weigh up risks in our efforts to be of service to others.

As you know, the Westgate Mall in Nairobi sustained a vicious attack in the past few days. I have been to Nairobi a few times before, but is it too dangerous to go there at this time? What are the risks? Is it worth it to go? What can I possibly offer that would make it worth it?

Well, I am going to work with a UN global project that is helping the urban and rural poor gain access to land and land security. That is important. How do I weigh up the risks in going?

Because there was a recent attack, perhaps it is less likely that there would be another one in just a few days. The authorities must be on special alert, so it may be even safer than usual. But who knows?

The people who live and work in Nairobi are going about their daily lives, so why shouldn't I be among them? But I don't have to, or do I? What is my motivation for going? How much of it is about service, how much about income, how much about ego, how much about risk-taking?

I read the alerts and cautions on the US State Department website. Basically, we are told to be careful. OK, we must do that anytime we cross the street. In fact, life is full of risks every day, all the time. We never know what might happen. It takes only a split second to damage or kill a fragile human organism. So, be careful.

So, do I go? It is just a choice. Well, I choose freely to go. I choose to live my life as a person who cares not only for his nation but also for all nations. And so I continue what I began over four decades ago when I started a journey that has now touched fifty-five countries around the world. Many years ago, I fell in love with a beautiful planet. Her name is Earth. And I fell especially in love with her earthlings—and of those, especially the humans.

They/we are so beautiful, mysterious, fragile, and glorious and so full of suffering and potential, love and hate, and truth and confusion. I go to Nairobi as a humble earthling to be among my brothers and sisters. And to get to go back again to East Africa where the first humans emerged—wow!—what an opportunity.

———

Worldly Power vs. Spiritual Power

Two types of power are at work in human society. Worldly power aims to control and dominate. This includes economic power, political power, cultural power, and environmental power. Spiritual power, on the other hand, intends to liberate and empower. Its essence is truth and love, wisdom and compassion.

Worldly power is motivated by pride and greed and uses fear, lies, hatred, and violence to subdue and control others. Spiritual power, however, is animated by goodwill and uses affirmation and peaceful means to help others realize their true nature.

Where do we see these two powers at work today? Worldly power is at work on Wall Street, in the big banks, in the fossil fuel industry, and with the 1 percent. Their objective is to secure and control capital and wealth at all costs to society or nature. We see worldly power in political elites. Their aim is to dominate democratic institutions by controlling media, voting laws, politicians, courts, and think tanks that write the laws. We see worldly power in cultural, racial, gender, and religious elites. Their intent is to negate and oppose the beliefs and behaviors of people who are different or part of a minority. We see worldly power of corporations and other institutions that harm the environment. Their way of being is to plunder and use up limited natural resources; pollute air, water, soil, plants, and animals; and spew carbon into the atmosphere without any regard for sustainability or concern for other living beings.

On the other hand, we see spiritual power in individuals who believe in interdependence and unity and exhibit kindness and generosity in their behavior with others. We see spiritual power in groups who maintain a culture of openness and universal human values of equality and justice and manifest compassionate action within communities, organizations, networks, policies, and systems.

Worldly power appears to be so massive and dominant. Is there any hope that spiritual power might ever prevail? Are there any historical examples or exemplars where spiritual power has overcome worldly power?

The Buddha, Jesus, and Mohammed, among others, lived lives of and taught others about love and truth. From their witness and example, millions and billions of people have and are attempting to live lives of compassion and wisdom. Mahatma Gandhi lived a life of and taught others about nonviolence and social justice, and his words and deeds have inspired millions around the world to do likewise. Martin

Luther King Jr. lived a life of and preached about equality, truth, and hope. His sacrifice changed attitudes and laws around the world.

In addition to these five male exemplars, there are the lives, deeds, and words of the many world-changing female leaders, saints, and revolutionaries. Today, we have Elizabeth Warren, among many others. Yesterday, we had Rosa Parks, Mother Teresa, Eleanor Roosevelt, Florence Nightingale, Susan B. Anthony, Saint Teresa of Avila, Mary Magdalene, and on and on.

And then there are the many amazing collective heroes: the Occupy movement, the labor union movement, the cooperative movement, the credit union movement, the democracy movement, the decentralization movement, the gift economy movement, the pay-it-forward movement, the fiscal reform movement, the human rights movement, the peace movement, the environmental movement, the green energy movement, the civil rights movement, the voter registration movement, the women's rights movement, the facilitation movement, the gay rights movement, the ecumenical movement, and on and on.

But is all of this enough to turn the tide of human history? The only questions you and I can and need to answer in relation to the seeming war between worldly power and spiritual power are as follows: Who am I? What do I do? How am I to be? Am I committed to pride and greed or kindness and generosity? And we answer these questions moment by moment with each word and deed.

In some moments, I let pride and greed take the lead; in other moments, I give kindness and generosity a turn. How can I strengthen my spiritual power so that I tend always toward kindness and generosity? Studying, meditating, contemplating, praying, participating in liturgy, practicing yoga, journal writing, going on retreats, being in good company, walking in nature, making vows, caring for those in need, being mindful, and relieving others' suffering—these are just a few of the many ways of increasing spiritual power.

Our challenge then is to use our spiritual power to transform worldly economic, political, cultural, and environmental power into kindness and generosity, sustainability and participation, tolerance and justice, equality and peace.

We can do this.

———

Dancing with Time

How Do We Live the Future Now?

It's all in the glance, the stance, and the dance.

What is really going on anyway? Have we moved beyond winning to win-win yet? How do we play an entirely different game? How do we step out of the old worldview and live in a completely new world?

The way I see it is that things are the way they are in the world because we humans create and maintain them that way with our thoughts, words, and actions. To change the collective assumptions and institutions of this confused world, you and I must wake up and change our individual minds and behaviors. How do we do that?

In a world committed to greed, we can manifest generosity. In a world aflame with anger and hatred, we can manifest peace and love. In a world trapped in rigid ego identity, we can manifest an interdependent, fluid self. In a world caught in a reification of the current social structures, we can manifest the truth of continuous transformation.

In a world self-satisfied with material comfort and accomplishment, we can manifest awareness of suffering and its relief by letting go of endless desire. In a world committed to violence, we can manifest nonviolence. In a world intolerant of differences, we can manifest understanding and compassion.

In a world premised on might makes right, we can manifest humility and solidarity with the least, the lost, and the last. In a world based on the repetition of lies, we can speak simply and factually.

In a world ruled by wealth and power, we can celebrate sufficiency and cooperation. In a world built on nonrenewable resources, we can treat Earth as sacred.

We can literally live this day in a different world—a world of the future and the realization of sustainability, equality, justice, participation, and tolerance. By embodying the values and behavior of this better world, we literally bring it into the present milieu of crises and collapse. The presence and energy of this new world become a magnet for positive emotions and actions, attracting around it greater and greater critical mass. As the old world implodes on itself, what remains is the new cultural and institutional architecture of a compassionate civilization.

Could this be the way we get from here to there, by bringing there to here and then to now, living as if it were already accomplished, realized, made new? Let's try it and see what happens.

And remember, it's all in the glance, the stance, and the dance.

What Are You Inventing with Your Life?

Even though the universe is 13.3 billion years old, because a human life lasts only one minute to 122 years, we tend to think in extremely short durations. How does this short-termism affect our decisions and actions? In politics, we think in two- to four-year periods because of election cycles, whereas the challenges we face often require ten- to one-hundred-year perspectives and coordinated solutions. Capitalists measure success in the stock market second by second.

Also, because a human body is so miniscule, we tend to think about the immediate space around us rather than the scale of planet

Earth or beyond. So, our imaginations are often trapped in a tiny bubble of space-time. And because we are so dependent for our existence on air, water, plants, animals, medicine, other people, institutions, and fiscal currencies, we are further trapped in worrying about our survival, hour by hour and day by day.

How can such a creature ever raise its head and sniff the infinite? Yet the philosophers among us have done so, as well as those we call scientists who have mapped the known universe of trillions of stars and its time-scape of billions of years of evolution. And yet we worry about what we will have for lunch, where we will get money to live, how we will get to work on time, and so forth.

How do we live this paradox between the immense and the immediate? How can the immense help us think beyond our tiny lives to at least encompass our city, our nation, and our planet? How can an understanding of the vast stretches of time in cosmic and planetary evolution help us deal with the long-term social, economic, political, cultural, and environmental challenges facing our species and all life on Earth?

I have found that motivation and perspective are released as we expand our context in every direction—our present, past, and future; our spatial sense; and our understanding of intention and energy. Expanding our sense of the future is especially important. We usually think about a day, a week, a month, a year, maybe two to five years, or at most twenty years. What if we started thinking about the next one hundred years, the next one thousand years, the next million years, or the next billion years? How would we act differently this day, in this moment?

I think that we would realize that what we choose to do in this very moment causes and affects all time. It is as though we are sending an energetic, causal ripple throughout space-time that is vast beyond imagining. This is how everything that we take for granted has come into being. This includes such notables as the big bang, the universe, the Milky Way, our sun-star, planet Earth, life itself, *Homo sapiens*, fire, the wheel, compassion, language, the city, democracy, the scientific method, and the theory of evolution, to name a few of the wonders of our lives.

And where and when does this creative act take place? Always in the present moment, that is the locus of our inventiveness and responsibility, and it touches everything and everyone.

What are you and I inventing with each thought and action of our lives? What ripples are we each setting in motion for all time? I hope that I am catalyzing a compassionate civilization by how I treat other living beings and how I walk lightly on this precious Earth, moment by moment. How about you?

———

The Divine Comedy: No Joke

What is the Divine Comedy?
Is it God's joke on us humans?
We are born, become conscious of all space and all time,
and then we die.
What is it all about—this life and death?
In this vast Cosmos, do we matter at all?
I like to think we do.
We are the Cosmos come conscious.

And that's a lot.

That is amazing.

That is worth being.

No joke.

And in our time and place, can we not love it all,

every creature great and small?

Yes, love is the way, the truth, the light.

Nothing else makes any sense to me whatsoever.

And that means everything.

Let's be our consciousness of this sublime mystery

in humility, gratitude, and compassion.

Spiraling, flinging out our star stuff for one and all.

———

You Are Bending History

How can we continue caring day after day without any assurance that what we are doing makes a difference in the grand sweep of history and evolution? We can realize that everyone's life happens in a particular here and a particular now and with particular people, and that this is the situation in which the challenge is presented to us of being relevant or not, of being ethical or not, of making a difference or not. Then, every encounter is experienced as a crisis or test of who we are and what we stand for.

Everyone who ever "changed history" or nudged evolution in a new direction did so in a particular moment, place, and circumstance. It was then and there that they manifested their intimate values and principles through the risk-taking of their own behavior and action. It was at that precise moment and location that cause and effect began to ripple outward. In that sense, everything we do makes a difference. But does it make a difference that makes a difference?

It does if we are fully present and invested in what we are doing, if we are manifesting our deep intention with our complete attention. As often quoted, Gandhi's admonition is to *be* the change we want for the world. I would add moment by moment, location by location, and situation by situation. Embodying vision and values is what it is all about. Walking the talk. Putting your life on the line. Going for broke. Holding nothing back. All or nothing. If not you, whom? If not now, when?

How you are parenting your children, treating your spouse, relating to your colleagues at work, or exercising your responsibilities as a citizen or a consumer makes a critical difference. Your choices and actions are creating the future of life on Earth. You can live your life on behalf of others or only for yourself. But whichever you choose, without you, the future will not be the same. You and I are more powerful than we would wish to acknowledge or be aware. What we do or do not do changes the world.

How Can We Change before It's Too Late?

Who are we humans? What are we? Who am I? What am I?

Today, these questions appeared once again. Always pregnant. Always empty. What is life about? What is my life about? The questions never stop and are answered only by living. My answer. Your answer. Our answer.

We are mammals. We are star stuff. We are consciousness. We are awake. We are love.

Why then are we so violent? No other life-form is as violent or with as much premeditation and justification of violence. No other life-form is as greedy or with such justification for greed.

Maybe we are a failed experiment. Maybe it is good that we are killing ourselves off by destroying the life-support systems of our planet. Maybe something will come after us that is more loving, more understanding, more tolerant, kinder, or wiser.

Or can we wake up in time—our time, now, here—and change our minds, our hearts, our actions, our cultures, or our institutions? Can I? Can you?

It's worth a try. No, it is worth everything to accomplish this, here, now. Then, we might have another century, millennium, one hundred thousand years, one million years, or even one billion years. It is worth changing myself and everything for that isn't it?

And how do I do that, here and now?

Practice meditation. Practice kindness. Practice forgiveness. Practice generosity. Practice compassion. Practice tolerance. Practice understanding. Practice openness. Practice patience. Practice peace. Practice equanimity. Practice justice. Practice equality. Practice sustainability. Practice trust. Practice transformation. Practice selflessness.

Practice, practice, practice as though your life, our life, and all life depends on it, because it does. And when you falter, which you will, then return to the practice, and practice some more.

———

Do We Have Time?

What is time? Is it a learned habit of referring to our human perception of past, present, and future? The other day, I saw an interview with a theoretical physicist on YouTube. He said that time may not be a fundamental characteristic of the universe. What could that possibly mean?

Our human experience is that some things are no longer happening and are therefore in the "past." Some things seem to be part of our lived "present." And then there are things that have not yet happened and are anticipated as part of a possible "future." But do these three segments of time "exist"? Or are they figures of speech concerning our experience of being part of an organic flow of continuous change, evolution, growth, and decay, as well as being in the midst of spatial distinctions and discontinuities?

How do we chat about time? "There's simply not enough time. I'm out of time. Time waits for no one. I had no time to spare. Time's up. How time flies! I did it in the nick of time. It was a timeless moment. Time stood still. They arrived ahead of time. It will be done all in good time or at a set time or from time to time. I was pressed for time. He lived on borrowed time."

Physicists tell us that before the big bang, there was no time. Before you were born, you were timeless; after you die, you will be out of time. Time may be an epiphenomenon of being a living, conscious being. It may be the way the brain makes sense of the change inherent in being and becoming.

How time flies! The year 2014 is almost one-twelfth over. How much time should there be in a lifetime anyway? Jesus was thirty-three when he was put to death. Dr. Martin Luther King Jr. was thirty-nine when assassinated. My wife Mary was sixty when she died of cancer. Pete Seeger was ninety-four when he died. Some people die as babies or children. What is long enough? Or is this the wrong question? Rather, should we ask, how intensely are we living our life? How authentically? With how much gratitude? Are we contributing our unique gifts to the civilizing process? Are we relieving others' suffering and making them happy? Are we giving all that we have and are? Are we loving each person and every moment of our lives?

This is our time. Let's use it well.

———

Who Are You, and What Time Is It?

Our lives take place in so many dimensions, sometimes sequentially, sometimes simultaneously. They all seem to be real yet are dramatically different. What does this tell us about our lives? What can we do about this? Should we choose the dimension that makes us happiest and let go of the others, or do we need to live them all with full passion and responsibility?

Sometimes, I am a grandfather. At other times, I am a professor. Then, I am a consultant, son, brother, father, husband, citizen, consumer, friend, and so forth. Are these all equally important? Am I called to be equally present in each of them? Is there a hierarchy of importance? Should they be prioritized?

There are only so many minutes in a day. I have only so much energy and attention. How should I live this multifaceted life? What difference does it make what I do, and to whom does it make a difference? What are my favorite roles? Least favorite? Most challenging?

Most natural? Whose approval am I most interested in receiving? Least interested? What is at stake here?

And this multifacetedness is going on at each stage of our lives as infants, toddlers, children, youth, young adults, adults, young elders, elders, and senior elders. It seems that we actually live many lives within many lives. What a mysterious journey! What complexity! What richness and diversity! And then it is over.

My grandparents have passed on, as have my parents. They can no longer give me their approval or withhold it. My early teachers no longer know what I am doing or have passed away. My friends don't really know who I am these days. My family members are closest, but they are so busy with their own lives. Those I interact with professionally continue to give me their feedback, for which I am grateful.

And what do I myself say about myself? Am I satisfied with who and what I am? Am I more of an admirer or a critic? What do I imagine archetypes or higher beings think of me? What could possibly be some criteria for being worthy of respect and appreciation? We all have our lists. Am I being responsible, kind, loving, helpful, generous, understanding, forgiving, and patient?

And so it goes. And then it ends or surely seems to. And then, the next generation of living beings has its time and turn. And it is good. It is all so deliciously, delightfully, deliriously good.

––––––––

What Is the Meaning of 2013?

A year is ending, and another is beginning. Or is it not just another miraculous day on planet Earth? We humans have our calendars and stories that we dearly love. And of course there are many different calendars and many different stories to provide meaning and sense to our lives. But then there is just the moment, the moment-to-moment aliveness of our lives. And what gives *that* meaning?

One of my earliest teachers often reminded us that life does not have a meaning (like icing on a cake); instead, life is its own meaning (it is the cake.) As beings who crave meaning, who interpret everything, and who have a story for every situation, we are always trying to discover the hidden meaning of our lives when it is staring us in the face with its "*is*ness."

Being alive and living our lives are their own mysterious meaning. I add "mysterious" because it reminds us that the meaning we live is not of our own making and defining but is given to us as an unknown and unknowable gift. We then give it a name, a category, a significance, an added *meaning*.

And what does any of this have to do with coming to the end of 2013 and anticipating 2014? How can we ever fully understand the year that we have just lived? How can we ever fully anticipate the year that awaits us, if indeed it does? But we crave to know, and so we add names, categories, significance, and meaning. We can do no less as we are essentially and incessantly meaning makers.

And yet, and yet, and yet...I would want for a moment to let go of that craving just for a moment and simply be in this moment, just be.

And when I am, what arises in my heart-mind?

Awareness arises.

Gratitude arises.

Mystery arises.

Compassion arises.

And this is sufficient as I let go of all the moments of 2013 and move into the first moments of 2014.

———

Embracing Sadness, Sickness, Old Age, and Death

I Am So Sad

I know it is the holiday season—a time of celebration, joy, gratitude, family, food, and gift giving. I hate to be a downer, but I am feeling so sad. When I look within, what do I find? Great sadness over being part of so much corruption and deception that does so much harm to so many. I cannot extricate myself from it. I am mired in it. It is inside me. It is me. It is my corruption and deception. It is harm that I carry out or is carried out in my name; with my tax dollars or investments; with my action, inaction, or impotence.

I am helping maintain a depraved system of lies and torture. Not just the CIA's torture but also the torture of Earth, women, children, native people, the poor, immigrants, and workers in sweatshops around the world. I have not personally engaged in waterboarding or beheadings, but I am part of a system that makes use of drones, air strikes, invasions, slave labor, unlivable wages, voter suppression, police brutality, hate crimes, and poisoning of the earth from extracting and burning fossil fuels.

I drive my car full of gasoline. I turn on electricity generated by dangerous nuclear energy. I am ensnared in a corrupt, deadly system. Yes, I could buy a used electric car. Yes, I can change the source of my electricity to wind or solar. But can I stop paying to feed the beast? Can I stop purchasing products made in sweatshops? Can I be so self-aware, so diligent, and so disciplined that I am free of guilt, free of the system? Or is it that no one has clean hands? We are all part of the global industrial-military empire.

How do I speak out, express my horror, separate myself from it, and cleanse myself of the blood and filth? I don't know. I will celebrate this holiday with my family. I will be happy. I will be grateful. But I will also be profoundly sad at so much suffering outside me and inside me. I will confess. I will grieve. I will do all that I can to relieve the suffering of all beings everywhere. This vow is my gift to the world and to myself. It is an impossible vow, but it is more real to me than anything else. May it be realized here and now and forever.

———

My Broken Heart

I cried in Grand Central on Saturday evening. I was standing in line to order a smoothie and panini after my all-day class at NYU. Someone behind me spoke, and I turned around. It was a young man, and he said that he was a disabled veteran and was hungry.

He asked me for some money and showed me his veteran documents. I asked him how he was going to improve his situation. He said that he was on a waiting list to get into some housing for disabled veterans. I looked in my wallet, and it was empty of cash. I looked in my briefcase and found eight dollars.

I asked him if he would rather I buy him a sandwich and drink because I could use a credit card. He said that he would rather buy a ninety-nine-cent sandwich at Burger King. I gave him the eight dollars and looked into his eyes. My eyes filled with tears, and in a choked voice, I said that I hoped that he would be all right.

He hugged me and thanked me from the bottom of his heart. I turned and ordered my smoothie of blueberries and yogurt. He walked away. I don't know if his story was true or not. I think that it was, but what if he needed drugs or were homeless for another reason? In any case, he was a person in need.

Of course there are millions of people who need help, who need food, who need housing, and who need a break. I think of the millions of Filipinos who are suffering tonight after the recent typhoon. How can we help? Yes, we should make a donation, but it is so little when the suffering is so vast and deep.

I know that we need to reinvent our societies so that they work for everyone and that everyone has opportunity, education, income, and a meaningful life. We need to stop burning fossil fuels that cause the formation of megastorms. We need to do so much, and meanwhile, people are suffering.

My heart is broken again and again, moment by moment. And yet I go on and do what I can to help others through my teaching, consulting, writing, speaking, and loving my family and friends. It is so little, but it is my gift given. May my heart remain broken. May compassion spill out in comfort and service to others.

———

We Shall Not Overcome If...

Sometimes, things feel pretty hopeless. Even with all our good intentions and heroic efforts, there is still enormous suffering all over our beautiful planet. As individuals, we can decide to be happy and hopeful, but the future can look pretty grim. How do we maintain our positive vision of what is possible and motivation to continue our work in spite of what we see and experience around us?

For example, after decades of efforts by the environmental movement, we don't see the dramatic shifts required for fossil fuel cessation and renewable energy investment; therefore, the earth continues to heat up with alarming consequences. We see an erosion of women's rights even after decades of significant legal and attitudinal advances. After a few centuries of democratic institutions, we see politicians, legislatures, courts, voting laws, and media being bought off by the wealthy. After millennia of religious teachings about love and compassion, we still see colossal armed conflict; degradation of the earth; and continuing violence perpetrated against people of a different race, ethnicity, religion, sex, or sexual preference. And after centuries of philosophical and political writings on equality and justice, we see staggering inequality of income and well-being of people.

How can we continue believing that it is possible to create a better world? Sometimes, it is hard. Yet continue we must. For the only way to ensure that the forces of greed and violence will succeed is to stop our efforts to create a better world for all. And we might stop if we assume either that there will be victory in any case and therefore our support isn't needed, or that victory will be lost regardless of what we do.

The one thing we can count on, however, is that things will change. If we continue believing and working, then we could prevail, and we might overcome. The fact is that ours is a time to intensify and expand our efforts on all fronts: climate change mitigation and adaptation, gender equality, participatory governance, cultural tolerance, and economic and social justice.

Things will change. The tide will turn. The ground will shift. The movement of movements can grow stronger and larger and alter the landscape of thought, law, behavior, and common sense. To this end, we rededicate ourselves this day and every day to practice hope, believe in possibility, and continue our activism, thus catalyzing the emergence of a better world, even a civilization of compassion.

————

Mindful of Old Age, Sickness, and Death

The Buddha began his spiritual awakening when, upon escaping the protected confines of his family palace, he encountered four phenomena for the very first time: an old person, a sick person, a dead person, and a monk. He suddenly realized that this life included suffering and impermanence and that there were ways to practice relating to the way life is.

After trying many spiritual paths and techniques and finding them all lacking, he finally sat down under a tree and simply became aware of his awareness. After some time, he fully awoke to the stunning realization that this life was indeed perfect and that there is a way to relieve all suffering. His realization was that by shining the light of mindfulness on suffering, impermanence, and interdependence, we could live this life in happiness, peace, compassion, and wisdom. What a staggeringly wonderful realization.

In a little over three months, I will celebrate living seven decades on planet Earth as this particular being. Every day, I become a little more aware of the inevitability of sickness, old age, and death. I think about my legacy. What have I already done? Is it enough? What else do I need to do in this life? When will I die? How long do I have?

I know that I could die at any moment. Of course that has always been true throughout my whole life. But now it seems more real, present, and urgent.

Every day, I dedicate myself to continually waking up to suffering, impermanence, and interdependence. I dedicate myself to relieving the suffering of all beings, including me. I dedicate myself to being compassionate and understanding. I dedicate myself to living a peaceful, happy life.

I dedicate myself to teaching, training, writing, consulting, and facilitating to awaken others to our time of crisis and opportunity; the possibility of an emerging civilization of compassion; and strategies and methods of innovative, creative, facilitative, integral leadership.

Is this enough? Can I do more? Can I love more? Can I give more?

And then it is over. And I am gone. And it is finished.

Yet, it goes on—humanity, life, this Earth, this Cosmos. And I am part of it forever, flowing onward, changing, awakening, and giving.

Gratitude.

Yes.

Getting Old Is Awesome!

World War II was ending. Another baby arrived under the sign of Leo in the Year of the Monkey—a boy child with white skin, brown eyes, and brown hair. He was born into a Protestant, middle-class, Midwestern American family—the beginning of the first decade.

Hey, I don't want to be seventy! It is far too old. I am not that old. I feel much younger. I am engaged, working, and traveling. I am healthy, happy, and connected. How can I be so old? Or is seventy old? Or is it eighty that is old? Or ninety? Or one hundred? Or 110? Or fifty? Or sixty? What is old? And what difference does it make anyhow? To me? To anyone?

In my seventieth year, I conducted an organizational development consultancy with a UN-Habitat global program on access to land for the poor involving two trips to Nairobi, Kenya; taught two New York University graduate courses (i.e., Innovative Leadership and International Capstone); made a keynote presentation at a symposium on creative peacemaking held at Oklahoma City University; taught a University of Aruba seminar for educational administrators on collaborative leadership; facilitated a workshop and made a presentation in the UN Public Service Global Forum on Sustainable Development held in Seoul, Korea; published eighty-seven blog posts on *A Compassionate Civilization*; and participated in Facebook, Twitter, and LinkedIn. Is that a lot? Is that a little? Is that enough?

But why don't I want to be seventy? I made it! I lived seven decades on planet Earth. I did it. I am alive and kicking. I still have work to do, being to be, and knowing to know. I am not finished. I am still here. They can't shut me up or put me on the shelf yet. I can sound off. I can tell the truth. I can be my being. I can be all that I can be, here and now. I can love. I can say, "I love you." Hip hip hooray!

I am proud of being seventy. Wow, seventy years of living on planet Earth. What a glory, what a gift, what an adventure, what a journey, what a learning. I am impressed with myself—to be turning seventy. Both of my grandfathers died in their midfifties. My two lovely grandchildren have a seventy-year-old grandfather. OK! They call me Grandpa Rob. I love it when they say that and look at me and ask me to play with them and ask me to put them to bed. I love being a grandpa. What a treat. I feel as if I get to be a kid again, to grow up again with my grandkids. And I get to be a parent again (sort of).

Someday, this body will cease to function altogether. I am learning to accept that. For now, it is quite miraculous that I am alive, conscious, thinking, moving, feeling, and relating. For this, I am grateful. I am happy. I am amazed. I am fascinated. In fact, I have only always experienced being alive. (As my colleague and author Joy Jinks says in her book *Dynamic Aging* in its subtitle "I intend to live forever, so far so good.") Yet I know that the universe was going on for 13.7 billion years before I was born and will go on for another several billion years after I die. What a mystery to wake up for this flickering moment and be conscious of all of it.

I am proud of my white hair and my wrinkles. Hey, this is what a human being looks like who has lived seventy years, OK? Pretty cool, huh? I watch what I eat. I exercise regularly. Get enough rest. Keep moving. Use it or lose it. Stay active. Stay involved. Stay connected. Keep learning, every day. Keep growing. Keep asking, "Why?" Keep being surprised. Keep smiling and laughing, especially at yourself—especially at myself. Keep being grateful. Keep risking and loving and feeling.

I love yellow, orange, and red. I love the sound of French horns. I love the shape of spiral galaxies. I love the photo of planet Earth from space. I love all kinds of flowers, buildings, and people's faces—all colors and shapes, and people's bodies—all sizes and shapes, and the sun, oh yes, the sun, and clouds, and on and on and on.

I love to eat; sleep; wake up; have my Bengal Spice tea, yogurt, and granola; say "Good morning" to my beloved wife; check my e-mail; take a hot shower; sit at my desk; and think and write. I love to dream about an emerging civilization of compassion. I love the happiness that is not a goal to be sought but a path to be walked, moment by moment.

In my seventieth year, I am profoundly grateful for my life; my wife; my two sons; my two grandchildren; my daughter-in-law; my brother; my two sisters-in-law; my brother-in-law; my nephews and nieces; my cousins; my aunt; and all my wonderful, loving family. I am forever grateful for my colleagues at the UNDP, UNDESA, and UN-Habitat; my colleagues and grad students at NYU; my ICA colleagues; my social artistry colleagues; and my friends. I am grateful for health, home, happiness, and my spiritual practice. I am grateful for loved ones who have passed on, including my late wife, my parents, my grandparents, and all my ancestors. I am grateful for my teachers, exemplars, and archetypes who have taught me, inspired me, encouraged me, and challenged me. I am grateful for planet Earth, the sun, the Milky Way, and this vast and mysterious universe.

I rededicate my life to relieve the suffering of all beings everywhere through concrete words and deeds. I will promote innovative leadership for sustainable human development, especially through teaching, training, facilitating, writing, and speaking. I vow to help catalyze the emergence of a civilization of compassion embodying environmental protection, gender equality, participatory governance, socioeconomic justice, and cultural tolerance and understanding. I commit the rest of my life to creating a world that works for everyone, in which each person can realize her or his full potential.

So, to paraphrase Margaret Mead, I say, "Thank God I'm me, and I'm seventy!" And as my grandchildren love to say (from *The Lego Movie*), "Everything is awesome!"

———

How Do We Keep Dancing?

Getting old is a bummer. This may seem to contradict my seventieth birthday reflection above, entitled "Getting Old Is Awesome!" But it doesn't. Both are true. These days, I am increasingly aware that the animal-body is falling apart little by little. Of course I am resisting mightily by going to the gym, eating well, taking supplements, meditating, getting sufficient sleep, teaching, writing, and being with loved ones. But aging seems to be inevitable, with death never so very far away. Today, I had six precancerous spots frozen on my face and one biopsied. Two years ago, I had surgery. Soon, I will need to take steps to improve my sight and hearing. And so it goes.

Two of my dear friends—a husband and wife—are ill, and one is not going to recover. It is hard. What to say? What to do? How to help? One is depressed, and the other is confused. Both are anxious. I have been visiting both of them and trying to be helpful. I understand their situation. I lost my first wife to cancer after thirty-five years of marriage; she was only sixty.

How do we dance this old-age jig of stiffness, pain, and anxiety? How do we keep smiling in the face of sickness and death? How do we continue to relieve suffering—others' and our own—and catalyze a compassionate civilization with our words and deeds? How do we enjoy the grandkids and encourage our young students?

We do so by keeping on keeping on, by not giving in to tiredness or depression, by daring to dream a new world, and by enjoying this fleeting life, moment by moment. Such delicious warmth of sunshine. What crisp, cold air. The laughter of happy grandkids. A shared meal with my sweetheart. The challenging questions of my students. Pushing aside the "But I don't feel like it." Reaching out, empathizing, and speaking encouragement with an energized voice and loving eyes.

Yes, we can. We can live this life to the end with dignity and passion. And the good news is we aren't dead yet! I could live one more day or thirty more years. Whatever it is, it is all good. Bring it on!

Impermanence

With open eyes and a joyous heart…How do we live with open eyes to the truth, the whole truth, and nothing but the truth and with a joyous heart?

Everything and everyone we love is passing away. We each die. The autumn air is cool and sweet, the colors are warm and earthy, and dry leaves float to the ground. It is beautiful. There is pathos. It is the way it is. Awareness. Gratitude.

Yet life surprises us with new life. Springtime! Babies! Yes!

Even the earth and the sun will cease to be in some distant future. That is the way it is. Civilizations rise and fall. Nations are born and cease to be and become part of something new. The atoms in our bodies are from stars. Changing, evolving...

But we have this moment, each moment, this aliveness, this awareness, this gratitude, and this joy. It is good to be alive even for a moment.

Earth is heating up. It is too late to stop the effects of that which we will suffer. We can stop further damage. But will we?

We can do better. We can be more compassionate and understanding. We can relieve suffering. We can create new structures that foster well-being and happiness for all living beings. But even these will be impermanent and will change. And so we try again. We never stop trying.

But what a gorgeous sunset, moonshine, and ocean glimmer. Beautiful eyes. The laughter of children.

Yes, my beloved, you and I are passing away, and I love you.

————

Dying Is So Very Natural

I never saw a wild thing
sorry for itself.
A small bird will drop frozen dead from a bough
without ever having felt sorry for itself.
("Self-Pity," poem by D. H. Lawrence)

Dying is as natural as breathing and eating. It is really the only way to make our exit from existing. We are born not by any merit or initiative of our own, and we die quite easily and swiftly at any moment when conditions are right. The true miracle is the life between birth and death. Breathing, eating, sleeping, thinking, talking, walking—it is all a miracle. How do we—well, most of us, that is—do it so effortlessly? For some, life's activities require huge effort and assistance and are even bigger miracles.

When loved ones die, it breaks our heart. We do not want to lose contact with their body and mind, their liveliness. But what we are left with is their absence and their presence. We have memories of lived moments with them, yet they are absent. But they are present in our mind and heart. When someone we love dies, it can make us more compassionate and wise. When we truly *know* that everyone dies, including us, we can be more patient, more understanding, and more loving.

When my wife died, I was so very sad. Then, I was confused, then angry, then lost, and then filled with a sick feeling of sorrow like a never-ending bout of fever and flu. These are the natural stages of grief. We must fully live them, experience them, accept them, work through them, let them change us, and let them evolve into something new. Grief work is very important. We mustn't hurry it, think it away, or shortchange it. It is healing us. It is giving rise to an increase of compassion and understanding of the mysteries of life and death.

Oh, but the hurt, the pain, the anxiety, the raw sense of loss. "Where art thou, my beloved? Where have you gone? Why did you leave me so soon? I miss you terribly. I love you so much."

After my wife died, we corresponded, and it helped me a little. I would write her letters on the computer, and she would write back with words of reassurance, comfort, and love. It helped a little, even though I knew that it was me writing back to myself on her behalf, imagining her mind, heart, and words. It helped me feel her love, her kindness, her wisdom, and her desire that I continue with my life, my service, and my mission.

What a mysterious gift we are given, this life and death.

————

What Is Worth Dying For?

Ten days ago, an old colleague of mine committed self-immolation. He wasn't an Asian monk but a Texas minister. He left messages explaining that he did this act as a protest against racism, capital punishment, and social injustice. He explained that he loved his life, was not depressed, and was not committing suicide but was making a final statement with his death as part of a long life lived for others. He was seventy-nine. I remember him as a wonderful combination of gentleness and passion. May his sacrifice wake each of us up to what is worth dying for.

Another old colleague of mine is in the midst of a march across America to call attention to climate chaos and the urgent necessity to stop burning fossil fuels and shift to renewable energy. He is seventy-seven. He is a strong-willed person who has lived a life of caring for others. May each of his steps from west to east wake each of us up to what is worth living and dying for.

Another elder colleague of mine goes to the streets of Albuquerque every day bringing food, clothing, and concern to the homeless. She is seventy-four. She is a brilliant, passionate person who has spent her life caring for others all over this world. May her loving expenditure wake each of us up to what is worth dying for, what is worth living for.

Each of these elders chose and chooses every day to do and to be what is worth living for and what is worth dying for. There is no single right answer. It is a deeply personal discernment and decision that we each must make in solitude and in community.

As for me, I have decided to engage in teaching, training, speaking, facilitating, and writing to promote innovative leadership for sustainable human development and to catalyze what I call a "compassionate civilization" of environmental protection, gender equality, participatory governance, socioeconomic justice, and cultural tolerance. This is not the right thing to do. It is what I am compelled to do with no assurance that it will make a difference.

Dying is a very lively part of life. What for you is worth living for and dying for? How might our living and our dying make a difference in another person's life, in society's perceptions and priorities?

A Reflective Structural Revolutionary

Yesterday, I saw an AARP video about a puppeteer. It was titled "It Is Enough to Know Who You Are?" So, I asked myself, "Who am I?"

I am a revolutionary. I want everything to change. I want to reinvent society. I want to catalyze a compassionate civilization. I want to create utopia here on Earth. That's who I am. I've spent my entire adult life trying to create a better world, first at the community-project level, then at the national- and global-policy level, and more recently at the individual educational level. I love what I do. I know who I am. How do I bring all three levels together in my final chapter?

But I'm the type of revolutionary who lives within the structures of society and who got married, had kids, got remarried, has grandkids, is a citizen of a country, and works within various organizations. I want to change structures from within, not from outside. I want to transform the system from within. That's me—the transestablishment, not the disestablishment or the establishment.

And so it goes, day after day, writing, teaching, training, facilitating, speaking, and demonstrating how it can be done.

I love this Earth. I love my family. I love myself. I love human society. I love great nature. I am saddened and weep as I experience social misery and environmental degradation. I am part of the movement of movements (MOM) that will transform everything and create a compassionate civilization.

And when my time is over, I will let go of this nondual nonself and become part of the endless revolution.

Writing the above makes me feel powerful, light, and happy. I am an incarnation, appearing for a moment to do a certain work and then disappearing. That is the way it works. That is what is supposed to happen. It is not a mistake. Suffering, sickness, old age, and death are not mistakes. They are part of the very essence of the sentient, nondual nonself. Otherwise, how would we ever learn compassion and wisdom, and how would we transform into what is needed next?

Ineffable mystery.

Gratitude upon gratitude.

———

EPILOGUE

Our Crisis, Our Challenge, Our Crusade

The arc of history is bent toward justice, equality, tolerance, participation, and sustainability. Today, however, we see the rising up of forces that oppose these trends and goals.

We see those full of fear and hatred fighting universal tolerance and respect for every belief and lifestyle. We see those drunk with greed fighting economic and social justice for all. We see the prideful fighting equal rights for women and the vulnerable. We see the powerful fighting participation of all in the political process. And we see the ignorant and shortsighted fighting sustainability and environmental protection.

Eventually, good must triumph over evil, right over wrong, tolerance over fear, justice over greed, equality over pride, and sustainability over destruction. But this victory will happen only if you and I and all persons of goodwill around this blue orb rise up and make it so, moment by moment.

This is our crisis. This is our challenge. This is our holy crusade.

———

It Is Time for the New Humans to Act

I have been wrong. I have thought that what is needed is the reinvention of human society, of human civilization. What I am coming to realize more and more is that what is needed is nothing less than the redefinition and reinvention of the human being itself. What is a human being? Who are we? What is our essence? What are our purpose and our destiny? We cannot merely be consumers and shoppers. We cannot merely be producers and salespersons. We are not merely citizens of the state. We are not merely animals. But what are we?

Sometimes, we seem so utterly depraved. We torture, murder, rape, destroy, and steal. We engage in wars that kill millions of people. We put people in gas chambers. We strangle unarmed citizens who are trying to make a living. We drop atomic bombs on helpless children, women, and men. We pollute the air, the waters, and the soil. We raise animals in tiny cages for our food. We annihilate whole species. We pump carbon into the atmosphere, bringing searing heat, megastorms, flooding, and droughts. The rich live in luxury while billions of people do not have food, water, toilets, and housing. Who are we? Are we devils?

Yet on the other hand, we sometimes seem so divine. We share with others. We give our lives for others. We give birth to others. We nurture, educate, and care for others. We create beautiful art, music, and dance. We invent magnificent theories about the universe, evolution, and the atom. We craft wonderful beliefs about love and truth, compassion and wisdom. We engage every day in billions of acts of kindness and understanding. We help the poor and heal the sick. We invent political systems that allow everyone to participate in self-governing. We create laws and policies that protect the weak and promote justice. We respect one another and honor differences of sex, culture, and religion. Who are we? Are we angels?

This has been the question for so very long. Are we humans half-way between heaven and hell—part angel, part devil? And which will we choose to embody and make manifest on this Earth? We have come so far from our caves, jungles, and savannahs. We have grown into a giant of over seven billion strong. We have erected great cities and connected humankind through the air and the airwaves. And what now? How do we wake up? How do we make the necessary leap? How do we transform ourselves? How do we die to who we have been and redefine and reinvent ourselves? And what is my role? And yours? How can you and I become the new human, and how can we together create the new society?

The new human knows that each moment is a moment of creation. I choose to be divine or depraved in each moment. I can act out of compassion, kindness, understanding, peace, and happiness, or I can act out of pride, greed, fear, anger, hatred, and violence. In each moment, we observe, reflect, interpret, decide, and act. That is it. That is how we reinvent the human being—by reinventing ourselves, moment by moment. And then the new humans together invent the new society, the new culture, the new institutions, and the new policies—the new civilization of compassion. There are already millions of new humans around this Earth. It is time for us to act.

———

Action Will Remove the Doubt

My grad students at NYU Wagner really liked this Chinese proverb that I introduced in our last strategic-management class: "Action will remove the doubt that theory cannot solve." After four weeks of creating mission statements and five-year visions, analyzing inhibiting and enhancing factors in the internal and external environment, and creating strategic directions and tactics, we finally came to action planning, implementation, and leadership. Suddenly, it all came clear. Aha, this is where we have been heading, where the rubber hits the road, when we decide what we each do Monday morning.

Participatory strategic management works. People feel ownership because they have helped create the plan. They are motivated to implement the action plan as the way to move toward their agreed-on five-year vision.

How could this methodology become the default setting in governance processes around the world? What if participatory strategic planning were used in legislative bodies at all societal levels—village, town, city, county, state, national, regional, and global—to design and implement policies, programs, and projects?

When I was a staff member at the UNDP, I facilitated strategic-planning workshops in global, regional, and national conferences, seminars, workshops, and retreats to formulate policies, design programs, create project plans, and reform institutions. It worked every time. Participants from the government, civil society, and the private sector were amazed how they could come together and in two days create a common vision, innovative strategies, and effective action plans that made sense.

Even before joining the UNDP, I facilitated strategic-planning events with national government agencies, private companies, not-for-profits, remote rural villages, and urban slums in the United States, Malaysia, South Korea, Jamaica, and Venezuela. And each time, action removed the doubt that theory could not solve.

Now is a time for action. We cannot continue theoretical debate concerning climate chaos, gender inequality, socioeconomic injustice, elitist governance, and cultural intolerance. We must act. We must stop extracting and burning fossil fuels. We must empower women and girls. We must ensure health and education for all people. We must provide jobs, a living wage, job training, and credit to everyone. We must strengthen the institutions of democracy that allow everyone to vote and participate in policy formulation. And we must protect the human rights of everyone regardless of religion, race, ethnicity, or sexual orientation.

Act now—vote, speak out, write, mobilize, organize, boycott, donate, volunteer, facilitate a multistakeholder strategic plan—and doubt will fade away.

―――――

Blessed Are the Children

I will close this book just as I opened it in the book's dedication—reflecting on my grandchildren and all children for thousands of years to come. May they live in a compassionate civilization! This reflection was written when I was in Nairobi a few years ago doing some consulting for UN Habitat.

This afternoon included a big treat for me. I got to Skype with Phoenix and Mariela, my two adorable grandchildren in Asheville, North Carolina. I showed them pictures of Nairobi, where I was, and they showed me the "books" that they have coauthored and coillustrated. I introduced my grandchildren to Paul, a Kenyan who works in the garden of this guest house. The grandkids danced and played. And their magnificent parents were also part of the conversation. What a blessing to get to grow up again with these beautiful children.

Phoenix has just lost his two front teeth. Guess what he wants for Christmas. He loves kindergarten, tap dancing, Lego bricks, and Ninja Kids Club. Mariela loves her ballet class and going to the gym with her mommy, Jennifer. This morning, Phoenix and his daddy, Christopher, went out to see the sunrise and to take photos, which they shared with me. They also shared a photo of the moon taken last night.

May all children everywhere be cherished and given every opportunity to be happy and to realize their full potential!

ADDENDUM: UN SUSTAINABLE DEVELOPMENT GOALS FOR 2030

Bibliography (for your further reading)

Publications

Berry, Thomas, and Brian Swimme.1994. *The Universe Story*. San Francisco: Harper One.

Bregman, Rutger.2016. *Utopia for Realists*. Amsterdam: The Correspondent.

Canfield, Jack, Mark Victor Hansen, and Jennifer Read Hawthorne. 2007. *Life Lessons for Loving the Way You Live*. Deerfield Beach: Health Communications.

Cheema, G. Shabbir, ed. 2003. *Reinventing Government for the Twenty-First Century*. Boulder: Kumarian.

Cheema, G. Shabbir, and Vesselin Popovski, eds.2010. *Engaging Civil Society*. Tokyo: UN University Press.

Dalai Lama, 14th.2001. *Ethics for the New Millennium*. New York: Riverhead Books.

Eisenstein, Charles. 2011. *Sacred Economics*. Berkeley: Evolver Editions.

Emmott, Stephen. 2013. *Ten Billion*. New York: Vintage.

Gandhi, Mohandas. 1993. *Gandhi: An Autobiography—The Story of My Experiment with Truth*. New York: Beacon.

Harman, Willis. 1990. *Global Mind Change*. New York: Grand Central.

Hock, Dee. 2000. *Birth of the Chaordic Age*. Oakland: Berrett-Koehler.

Houston, Jean. 1982. *The Possible Human*. Los Angeles: J. P. Tarcher.

King, Martin Luther, Jr. 2010. *Strength to Love*. Minneapolis: Fortress.

Klein, Naomi. 2017. *No Is Not Enough*. Chicago: Haymarket Books.

------------------2014. *This Changes Everything: Capitalism vs. the Climate*. New York: Simon & Schuster Paperbacks.

Kolbert, Elizabeth. 2014. *The Sixth Extinction: An Unnatural History*. New York: Henry Holt.

Korten, David C. 1995. *When Corporations Rule the World*. Boulder: Kumarian and Berrett-Koehler.

Lawrence, D. H. 1959. *Selected Poems*. New York: Viking Compass.

Mandela, Nelson. 1995. *Long Walk to Freedom*. New York: Back Bay Books.

McKibben, Bill. 2011. *Eaarth: Making a Life on a Tough New Planet*. New York: St. Martin's Griffin.

Nhat Hanh, Thich. 1998. *The Heart of the Buddha's Teachings*. Berkeley: Parallax.

Reich, Robert B. 2016. *Saving Capitalism*. New York: Vintage.

Rifkin, Jeremy. 2009. *The Empathic Civilization*. New York: J. P. Tarcher/Penguin.

Sanders, Bernie. 2016. *Our Revolution*. New York: Thomas Dunne Books.

Stanfield, R. Brian. 2000. *The Art of Focused Conversation*. Toronto: The Canadian Institute of Cultural Affairs.

_____2002. *The Workshop Book*. Toronto: The Canadian Institute of Cultural Affairs.

Staples, Bill. 2012. *Transformational Strategy*. Toronto: Canadian Institute of Cultural Affairs.

Teilhard de Chardin, Pierre. 1959. *The Phenomenon of Man*. New York: Harper Colophon Books.

Timsina, Tatwa. 2012. *Changing Lives, Changing Societies*. Kathmandu: ICA Nepal.

United Nations Development Programme. 2012. *Human Development Report 2011*. New York: Palgrave Macmillan/United Nations.

Warren, Elizabeth. 2014. *A Fighting Chance*. Metropolitan Books, New York.

Wilber, Ken. 2007. *The Integral Vision*. Boulder: Shambhala.

Williams, R. Bruce. 2006. *More Than 50 Ways to Build Team Consensus*. Thousand Oaks: Corwin.

Work, Robertson. 2007. "Strengthening Governance and Public Administration Capacities for Development: A UN Background Paper." New York: United Nations.

Yousafzai, Malala. 2015. *I Am Malala*. New York: Back Bay Books.

Websites

350.org

ACLU, www.aclu.org

A Compassionate Civilization (blog,) http://compassionatecivilization.blogspot.com/

Big History Project, www.bighistoryproject.com/home

Charter for Compassion, www.charterforcompassion.org

Democracy Now, www.democracynow.org/

Democracy Spring, www.democracyspring.org

Disruption, watchdisruption.com

Emberling, Dennis. 2005. "Stages of [Leadership] Development." www.developmentalconsulting.com/pdfs/Stages_of_Development_vA.pdf

Greenpeace, www.greenpeace.org/international/en

Gross National Happiness, http://www.gnhcentrebhutan.org/what-is-gnh/

Human Rights Watch, www.hrw.org

IndivisibleGuide.com, www.indivisibleguide.com

Institute of Cultural Affairs (ICA) International, www.ica-international.org

Integral Institute, in.integralinstitute.org/integral.aspx

International Association of Facilitators (IAF), www.iaf-world.org/site

Kosmos, www.kosmosjournal.org

New York University (NYU) Wagner Graduate School of Public Service, wagner.nyu.edu

One World House, oneworldhouse.net

Our Revolution, ourrevolution.com

Pale Blue Dot, www.youtube.com/watch?v=p86BPM1GV8M

Peoples Climate, peoplesclimate.org

People's Summit, www.thepeoplessummit.org

Social Artistry, www.jeanhouston.org/Social-Artistry/social-artistry.html

Technology of Participation (ToP) Network, icausa.member clicks.net

The Story of Solutions, www.youtube.com/watch?v=cpkRvc-sOKk

Transition Towns, www.transitionus.org/transition-towns

Trusted Sharing, www.trustedsharing.com

UN Department of Economic and Social Affairs (UNDESA), www.un.org/development/desa/en

UN-Habitat, unhabitat.org

United Nations Development Programme, www.undp.org

United Nations Sustainable Development Goals, www.un.org/sustainabledevelopment/sustainable-development-goals

Universal Declaration of Human Rights, www.un.org/en/universal-declaration-human-rights/

INDEX OF INDIVIDUAL REFLECTIONS

ABOUT THE AUTHOR

ROBERTSON WORK is an international development prac-
titioner who has worked in over fifty countries worldwide.
Currently, he is a professor of innovative leadership and strategic
management at New York University (NYU) Wagner Graduate
School of Public Service; UN consultant; Fulbright Specialist; writ-
er; public speaker; activist; and adviser to Trusted Sharing, a social
media start-up. As the United Nations Development Programme's
principal policy advisor on decentralized governance for sixteen
years, Work assisted many developing countries in formulating new
policies and programs. While with the nonprofit Institute of Cultural Affairs (ICA) for twenty-one years, he led numerous commu-

nity, organizational, and leadership development projects in several countries. Work has contributed to eleven books. He received his bachelor of arts in English from Oklahoma State University, which honored him with the Distinguished Alumnus Award in 2003, and his graduate studies were at Indiana University and Chicago Theological Seminary. He and his wife live in Asheville, North Carolina, and Garrison, New York. More information about Work can be found at https://wagner.nyu.edu/community/faculty/robertson-work, and www.linkedin.com/in/robertsonwork.